THE "FIRST STAGE" GUITAR BOOK
Learn How To Play Guitar Easily & Quickly!

Created By...C. F. Lopez, Jr. 'Chris'

Welcome to **The "First Stage" Guitar Book!** This guitar book contains a simple method that will help you to master the skill of playing the most commonly played guitar chords quickly and easily without having to learn anything about music theory, so that you can enjoy playing your favorite guitar songs right away.

You will discover that this guitar chord book will not overwhelm you with more chords than you need to know at this early stage of learning to play the guitar, however will provide you with only the essential guitar chords in a simplified method.

I begin with diagrams of chord combinations in "open" chord form, followed by the same chord combinations in "barre" chord form. This will make it possible to play the same chord in two different finger patterns and positions on the guitar neck.

After the series of the most commonly played "open" guitar chords, you will find a very useful chord combination chart which will enable you to create many more chord combinations of your choice.

You will find that by focusing and learning the most commonly played guitar chords, you will be on your way to playing the songs you enjoy as well as your own creations a lot sooner.

There are also a few basic practice scale patterns with chord progressions to go with them at the back of the book so you can get a feel of what it is like to play lead guitar.

D0817157

New & Revised July 2001

ISBN 0-9667719-6-6

Printed in the United States of America

The "First Stage" Guitar Book
Learn How To Play Guitar Easily & Quickly!

Acknowledgement

Special thanks to Russ Hucek, President of Kradl, Inc., maker of the new and the uniquely designed KRADL® Guitar Picks, for his contributions and professionalism in guitar playing and instruction techniques.

www.KradlDirect.com

Book Cover Design
Lyndon Vasquez
E-mail: studiolv@hotmail.com

THE "FIRST STAGE" GUITAR BOOK
Learn How To Play Guitar Easily & Quickly!

TABLE OF CONTENTS

Christopher Winkle Products
P.O. Box 1898, Lomita, California 90717 USA
E-mail: quickstartguitar@msn.com

GETTING STARTED

Before getting started, I have included some general information about the guitar:

*   **Tuning The Guitar:** The best way to tune the guitar is by using any number of quality pitch pipes, tuning forks or battery powered guitar tuners which are available at many fine music stores.

*   **Guitar Pick:** For beginners, a light or medium gauge (thickness) pick is suggested because they offer more flexibility (and less resistance) when strumming chords. Hold the pick in such a manner that the tip of the pick points slightly upward when strumming downward across the strings. Conversely, when strumming upward, allow the tip of the pick to aim slightly downward.

*   **Positioning The Guitar:** Rest the curve section (the waist) at side of the guitar comfortably on the lap of your right leg, behind your knee. Hold the neck up in a slight angle with the left hand.

*   **Positioning The Left Hand On The Guitar Neck:** Grab the guitar neck with your left hand so that the thumb is positioned behind the neck and resting comfortably against it. Your finger tips should be resting on the strings. Avoid "choking" the neck with excessive force. Try to keep your left hand relaxed.

GETTING STARTED

*   <u>Positioning The Fingers On The Guitar Neck</u>: Press left hand finger **TIPS** near (but NOT on) the frets (the fret wire) when playing the chords. Apply a firm, downward pressure against the strings. It is important that you use your **FINGER TIPS** when playing and **NOT** the fleshly part of your finger that lies between the tip of your finger and the first knuckle. Finger tips may become sore at first, but this discomfort will lessen with time and practice.

*   <u>Strumming The Strings</u>: Strumming is the technique used to play chords (three or more notes) with the pick. To begin the strum, start with the lower (in pitch) or heavier strings at the top, as you look down at your guitar. While you hold a chord with your left hand, strum downward across all the strings in the chord. Slowly, or at a speed that is comfortable for you, practice strumming **<u>each</u>** chord at least four (4) times. Practice keeping time by tapping your foot and counting to four (1 anna, 2 anna, 3 anna, 4, etc.). Every time you count the "number," a strum should coincide with your foot tapping the floor. The "anna" should coincide with your foot completely raised off the floor. Once the downward strum is mastered, practice a strum that uses both the downward strum and an upward strum. In this instance, the downward strum "plays" the "numbered" count and the upward strum "plays" the "anna" count.

*   <u>Power Chords</u>: Power chords are created when you vigorously strum down on the lowest first two or three strings of a chord, usually the 6th, 5th, and/or 4th strings of a chord (thickest strings).

HOW TO TUNE YOUR GUITAR

The best way to tune the guitar is by using any number of quality pitch pipes, tuning forks or battery powered guitar tuners which are available at any fine music store.

It is critical that you keep and play your guitar "in tune." Another important, but often overlooked point, is to learn which tuning peg tunes which string, and the direction you have to turn the pegs to raise and lower the pitch of the strings. Learning this very mechanical aspect of the guitar will save you much time and confusion now and in the future. One last fine point about tuning; always tune your guitar so that you are **raising** the pitch to the correct note. That is to say, you should be **tightening** the strings as you tune your guitar, as opposed to loosening the strings, to achieve the desired note. This practice eliminates "slippage" or the slack that occurs when tension on a string(s) is lessened, causing the string to quickly go out of tune again.

* Please, take note of the arrows in the diagram on the following page. One end of the arrow points to the note which is to be held down (with the second finger) during the tuning process. The other end of the same arrow points to the open string which will be tuned to the note that is being held down at the opposite end of the arrow.

HOW TO TUNE YOUR GUITAR

BELOW THE DIAGRAMS ARE THE STRING NOTE NAMES AND THE CORRESPONDING STRING NUMBERS.
* BEGIN BY TUNING THE 6TH STRING- THE OPEN LOW "E" NOTE (TO A LOW "E" NOTE PITCH)

"OPEN" MEANS:
THE STRING IS NOT PRESSED DOWN

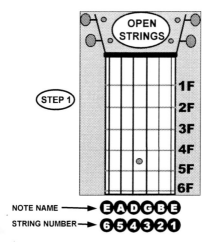

STEP 1

OPEN STRINGS

1F
2F
3F
4F
5F
6F

NOTE NAME → Ⓔ Ⓐ Ⓓ Ⓖ Ⓑ Ⓔ
STRING NUMBER → ❻ ❺ ❹ ❸ ❷ ❶

PLACE YOUR MIDDLE FINGER AND PRESS DOWN ON THE 5TH FRET-6TH STRING, STRIKE THIS NOTE (THIS IS AN "A" NOTE). NEXT, STRIKE THE OPEN 5TH STRING (THE OPEN "A" NOTE STRING), <u>TUNE THE OPEN "A" NOTE STRING TO THE PITCH OF THE NOTE BEING HELD DOWN WITH YOUR FINGER.</u>
BOTH STRINGS SHOULD MATCH IN PITCH.
(TO AN "A" NOTE PITCH)

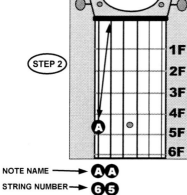

STEP 2

"A" Notes

1F
2F
3F
4F
Ⓐ 5F
6F

NOTE NAME → Ⓐ Ⓐ
STRING NUMBER → ❻ ❺

PLACE YOUR MIDDLE FINGER AND PRESS DOWN ON THE 5TH FRET- 5TH STRING, STRIKE THIS NOTE (THIS IS A "D" NOTE). NEXT, STRIKE THE OPEN 4TH STRING (THE OPEN "D" NOTE STRING), <u>TUNE THE OPEN "D" NOTE STRING TO THE PITCH OF THE NOTE BEING HELD DOWN WITH YOUR FINGER.</u>
BOTH STRINGS SHOULD MATCH IN PITCH.
(TO A "D" NOTE PITCH)

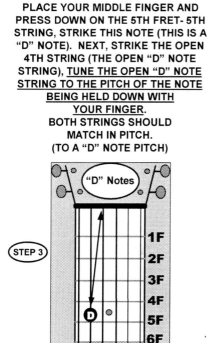

STEP 3

"D" Notes

1F
2F
3F
4F
Ⓓ 5F
6F

NOTE NAME → Ⓓ Ⓓ
STRING NUMBER → ❺ ❹

PLACE YOUR MIDDLE FINGER AND PRESS DOWN ON THE 5TH FRET-4TH STRING, STRIKE THIS NOTE (THIS IS A "G" NOTE). NEXT, STRIKE THE OPEN 3RD STRING (THE OPEN "G" NOTE STRING), <u>TUNE THE OPEN "G" NOTE STRING TO THE PITCH OF THE NOTE BEING HELD DOWN WITH YOUR FINGER.</u>
BOTH STRINGS SHOULD MATCH IN PITCH.
(TO A "G" NOTE PITCH)

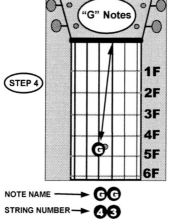

STEP 4

"G" Notes

1F
2F
3F
4F
Ⓖ 5F
6F

NOTE NAME → Ⓖ Ⓖ
STRING NUMBER → ❹ ❸

PLACE YOUR MIDDLE FINGER AND PRESS DOWN ON THE 4TH FRET-3RD STRING, STRIKE THIS NOTE (THIS IS A "B" NOTE). NEXT, STRIKE THE OPEN 2ND STRING (THE OPEN "B" NOTE STRING), <u>TUNE THE OPEN "B" NOTE STRING TO THE PITCH OF THE NOTE BEING HELD DOWN WITH YOUR FINGER.</u>
BOTH STRINGS SHOULD MATCH IN PITCH.
(TO A "B" NOTE PITCH)

STEP 5

"B" Notes

1F
2F
3F
Ⓑ 4F
5F
6F

NOTE NAME → Ⓑ Ⓑ
STRING NUMBER → ❸ ❷

PLACE YOUR MIDDLE FINGER AND PRESS DOWN ON THE 5TH FRET-2ND STRING, STRIKE THIS NOTE (THIS IS AN "E" NOTE). NEXT, STRIKE THE OPEN 1ST STRING (THE OPEN "E" NOTE STRING), <u>TUNE THE OPEN "E" NOTE STRING TO THE PITCH OF THE NOTE BEING HELD DOWN WITH YOUR FINGER.</u>
BOTH STRINGS SHOULD MATCH IN PITCH.
(TO AN "E" NOTE HIGH PITCH)

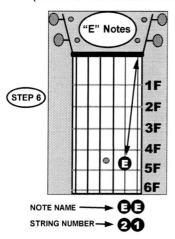

STEP 6

"E" Notes

1F
2F
3F
4F
Ⓔ 5F
6F

NOTE NAME → Ⓔ Ⓔ
STRING NUMBER → ❷ ❶

GUITAR STRING NOTE NAMES

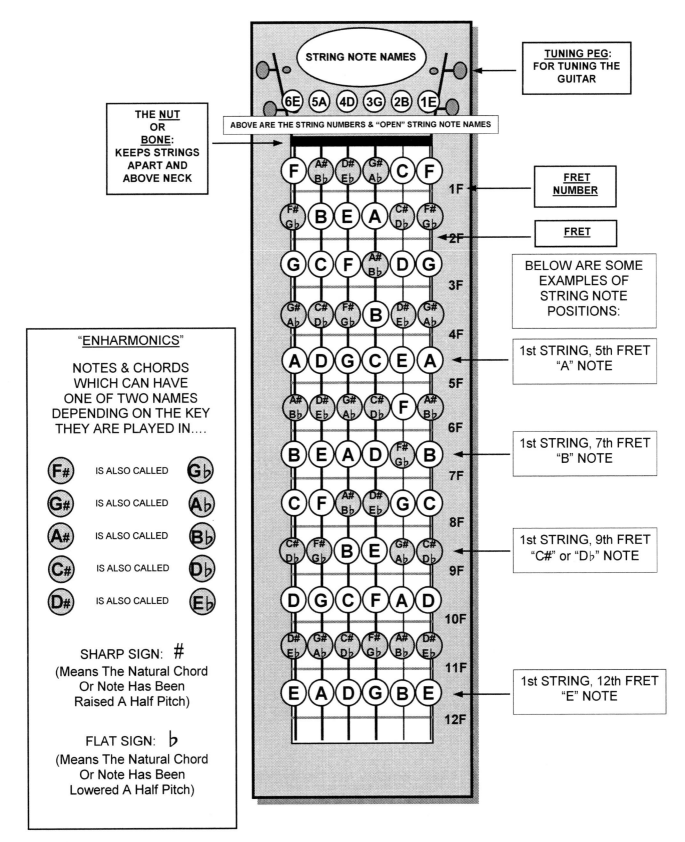

PRACTICE & PATIENCE ARE THE KEYS
TO SUCCESSFULLY LEARNING TO PLAY THE GUITAR

THE STAFF & NOTE NAMES

Standard musical notation is written on a **"Staff."** The staff is comprised of five (5) horizontal lines and four (4) horizontal spaces between the five lines. These lines and spaces make up the staff where music notation or notes are written.

There are seven (7) notes named after the first seven (7) letters of the alphabet **(A-B-C-D-E-F-G).**

To determine the name and pitch of the notes, a clef sign is placed at the very beginning of the staff. There are several different clefs for various instruments. The guitar uses the **"G"** or **Treble Clef.** The treble (G) clef resembles an ampersand ("&").

This is technical stuff, but notes can be played "Natural" (A - B - C - D - E - F - G), or notes can be altered from there natural state. That is to say a note(s) can be raised or "sharpened" (#) above its natural position. Conversely, the same note(s) can be lowered or "flattened" (♭) below its natural position. The **Key Signature,** with the use of sharps and flats, will determine what "key" a scale (or song) is in. The **Key Signature** is the area immediatley to the **RIGHT** of the **Treble ("G") Clef.** The absence of sharps or flats means the scale is written in the Key of "C" Major (or A minor, a "related" key to "C" major). The presence of sharps or flats means the scale or song is written in a key other than the Key of "C" (i.e., one sharp = the Key of "G," one flat = the Key of "F"). If the song is written in the Key of "G," then **ALL** your "F's" will be sharp. If the song is written in the Key of "F," then **ALL** your "B's" will be flat. Other Keys will have more notes that are either sharp or flat. The staff on the next page shows where the individual notes are located on the guitar. You will find more and illustrations of **Key Signatures** in *The "Next Stage" Guitar Book – Learn How To Play Scale Patterns & Tabs Easily & Quickly!*

THE STAFF & NOTE NAMES

Hint: Remember that the **LINE NOTES** on the staff use the first letter of each word in the saying: **"Every Good Boy Does Fine"** (E-G-B-D-F), while the **SPACE NOTES** on the staff spell the word **"Face"** (F-A-C-E). You will also notice that any given note can and does reside on both the Lines and Spaces (i.e., "E" is a line note in "Every Good Boy Does Fine" and a space note in "FAC**E**").

REFER TO THE "GUITAR STRING NOTE NAMES" DIAGRAM ON PAGE 10 TO LOCATE EACH OF THE NOTES BELOW. THE SMALL BOXES BELOW THE NOTES INDICATE WHERE THE NOTES ARE LOCATED ON THE GUITAR NECK. FOR EXAMPLE THE BOTTOM "E" NOTE IS LOCATED ON THE 6TH STRING, THE STRING IS PLAYED AS AN "OPEN STRING". THE "A" NOTE ON THE 2ND SPACE OF THE STAFF IS LOCATED ON THE 3RD STRING, 2ND FRET.

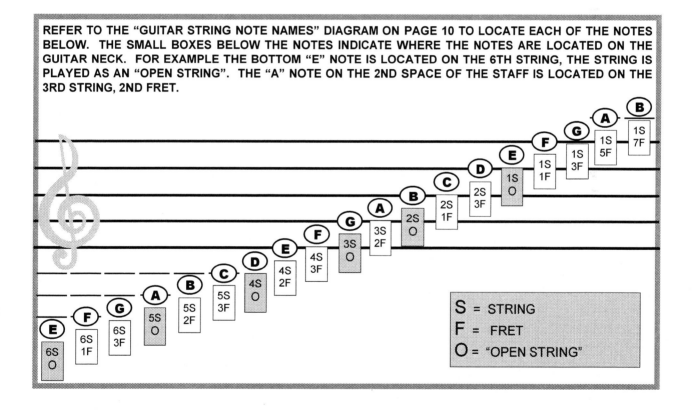

LEFT HAND FINGER POSITIONING

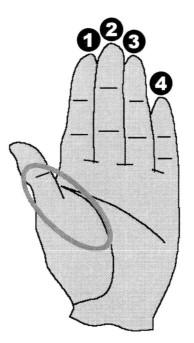

* AS SHOWN ABOVE, THE LEFT HAND FINGERS ARE NUMBERED SO YOU WILL KNOW WHERE EACH FINGER IS TO BE PLACED ON THE GUITAR NECK FINGERBOARD: NUMBER 1 (INDEX FINGER), NUMBER 2 (MIDDLE FINGER), NUMBER 3 (RING FINGER), NUMBER 4 (PINKY FINGER).

* DO NOT GRIP GUITAR NECK, BUT "REST" CIRCLED PORTION OF THUMB AND PALM ON BACK NECK OF GUITAR. SO THAT THE REST OF THE PALM WILL ARCH MUCH BETTER, ALLOWING FINGER TIPS TO AIM DOWN AS STRAIGHT AS POSSIBLE SO THAT THEY WILL REST FIRMLY ON NUMBERED GUITAR STRINGS ONLY AND NOT TOUCH OTHER STRINGS.

* SLOWLY OR MODERATELY STRUM <u>EACH</u> CHORD YOU PLAY AT LEAST FOUR TIMES, TO A COUNT OF FOUR, TRY TAPPING YOUR FOOT TO KEEP COUNT (1 ANNA 2 ANNA 3 ANNA 4), OR UNTIL YOU FIND WHAT IS COMFORTABLE FOR YOU. (THE "NUMBER" COUNT IS WHEN YOUR FOOT TAPS THE FLOOR, THE "ANNA" COUNT IS WHEN YOUR FOOT IS RAISED).

<u>A CLEARER SOUND WILL SOON BE PRODUCED WITH PRACTICE</u>

<u>BE SURE TO PLAY ALL "OPEN STRINGS" IN THE CHORDS ALONG WITH THE NUMBERED FINGER STRINGS!</u>

X = <u>DO NOT PLAY BROKEN LINE STRINGS IN CHORD DIAGRAMS!</u>

LET'S GET GOING!
(3 Finger Easy Practice Start-Up Chords)

LET'S GET GOING!
(3 Finger Easy Practice Start-Up Chords)

BELOW ARE THE OPEN GUITAR CHORDS I RECOMMEND FOCUSING ON AS THE FIRST GROUP OF CHORDS YOU SHOULD BEGIN TO PRACTICE OVER AND OVER UNTIL YOU ARE ABLE TO MOVE FROM ANY ONE OF THESE CHORDS TO ANOTHER FROM MEMORY AND EASE. THIS REPETITION WILL PREPARE YOU TO LEARN OTHER CHORD PROGRESSIONS (CHORD TO CHORD MOVEMENTS) LATER ON AS YOU MOVE ON TO LEARN "BARRE CHORDS," "7TH CHORDS," "9TH CHORDS," AND OTHER FORMS OF CHORDS.

WHAT IS SO NEAT ABOUT LEARNING THESE CHORDS IS THAT ALL OF THESE CHORDS WILL WORK TOGETHER AND THEY ARE SOME OF THE MOST COMMONLY PLAYED CHORDS. ANOTHER REASON IS THAT YOU WILL NOT HAVE TO CONCERN YOURSELF WITH WHAT CHORD GOES WITH WHAT CHORD, SIMPLY BEGIN TO PRACTICE ANYONE OF THESE CHORDS AND JOIN IT WITH ANY ONE OR MORE OF THE OTHER CHORDS YOU CHOOSE. (SEE PAGE 14 FOR FINGER PLACEMENT)

PLACE APPROPRIATE FINGERS ON ALL THE NUMBERED STRINGS. NOTICE THAT SOME OF THE NUMBERED STRINGS ARE GRAY COLORED, AS YOU ARE STRUMMING THE COMPLETE CHORD, PRACTICE LIFTING THE GRAY COLORED NUMBERED FINGER UP AND DOWN ON THE CHORD AS YOU STRUM, YOU WILL FIND THAT THIS TECHNIQUE WILL ADD AN ENHANCING SOUND TO THE CHORD.

SLOWLY OR MODERATELY STRUM EACH CHORD YOU PLAY AT LEAST FOUR TIMES, TO A COUNT OF FOUR, TRY TAPPING YOUR FOOT TO KEEP COUNT (1 ANNA 2 ANNA 3 ANNA 4), OR UNTIL YOU FIND WHAT IS COMFORTABLE FOR YOU. (THE "NUMBER" COUNT IS WHEN YOUR FOOT TAPS THE FLOOR, THE "ANNA" COUNT IS WHEN YOUR FOOT IS RAISED).

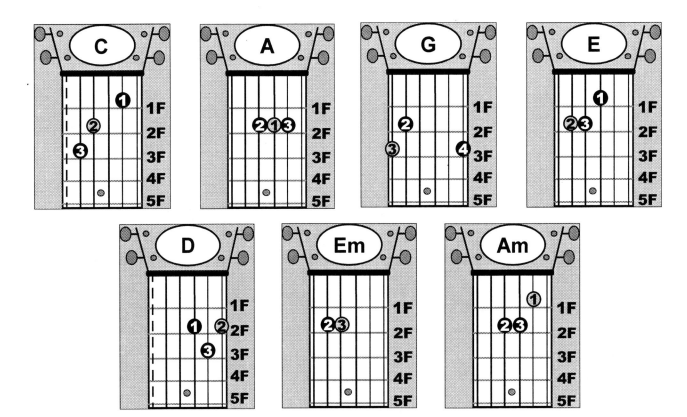

HERE'S A CLEVER WAY TO MEMORIZE THESE CHORDS, TAKE THE FIRST LETTER OF EACH CHORD AND NOTICE THAT THEY SPELL OUT THE PHRASE "CAGE DEA" KEEPING IN MIND THAT THE LAST TWO LETTERS OF THE LAST TWO CHORDS ARE MINOR CHORDS.

LET'S GET GOING!
(3 Finger Easy Practice Start-Up Chords)

HERE ARE JUST A FEW CHORD COMBINATIONS THAT ARE TAKEN AND PUT TOGETHER FROM THE PRACTICE CHORDS ON PAGE 14A. (STRUM THESE CHORD GROUPS AS DESCRIBED ON PAGE 14A)

YOU CAN FORM SOME OF YOUR OWN COMBINATIONS SO THAT YOU CAN PRACTICE MOVING FROM CHORD TO CHORD WITH EASE, REPETITION AND PRACTICE ARE THE KEYS HERE, IN TIME, IT WILL BECOME EASIER AND EASIER AND YOU WILL BEGIN TO UNDERSTAND WHY IT WAS RECOMMENDED TO LEARN THE CHORDS ON PAGE 14A. (TWO OTHER CHORDS THAT ARE RECOMMENDED TO LEARN AT THIS EARLY STAGE ARE THE "F" Chord-Page 44 AND THE "Dm" Chord-Page 46)

1ST CHORD GROUP

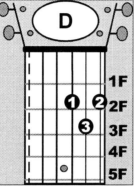
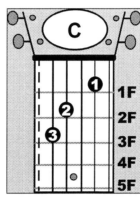
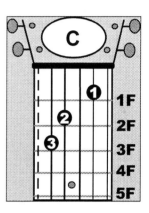

2ND CHORD GROUP

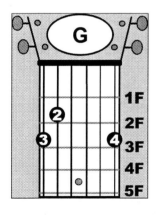

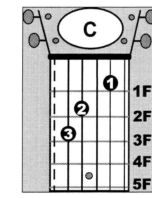
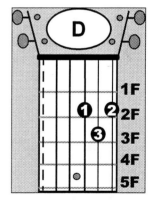

3RD CHORD GROUP

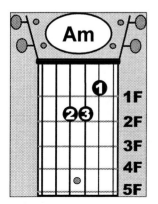
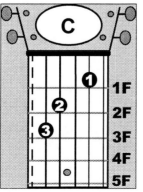
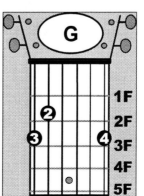
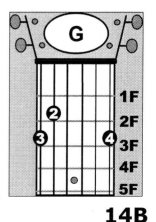

14B

"OPEN" & "BARRE" CHORD COMBINATIONS!

"OPEN" & "BARRE"
CHORD COMBINATIONS

All music originates from the "Chromatic Scale" (the Musical Alphabet, i.e., A, B, C, D, E, F, G) which consist of twelve successive notes which follow a specific order, i.e., A, (A# or B♭), B, C, (C# or D♭), D, (D# or E♭), E, F, (F# or G♭), G, (G# or A♭) and then you begin with A again and the order repeats itself over and over-the successive order of notes can begin with any one of the notes). Chromatic scales can easily be built on the guitar neck, for instance a chromatic scale for the 1st String, beginning with the open "E" Note, would be: E, F, F#, G, G#, A, A#, B, C, D, D#, E. (See Page 10 "Guitar String Note Names" Diagram)

Whenever you are moving a specific chord finger pattern up or down the neck, only the first letter of the chord name will change, that first letter of the new chord will follow the same successive order of notes as indicated in the musical alphabet. If you wish to move a chord, be sure to keep the finger pattern of that chord on the same strings as you move it up or down the guitar neck, only the first letter of the chord name will change as you move the chord (i.e., Fm Chord, F#m Chord, Gm Chord, G#m Chord and so forth-chords which have extensions, that would be any additional letters or numbers that follow after the first letter of the chord name (i.e., Fm-the extension to this chord is the "m" (minor), Cmaj7-the extension to this chord is the "maj7", G7-the extension to this chord is the "7" and so forth). The "extensions" of any chord will remain the same on the chord you are moving, again, the only part of the chord that will ever change will be the first letter of the chord.

ALL GUITAR CHORDS ARE MADE UP OF AT LEAST THREE MUSICAL NOTES FROM THE MUSICAL ALPHABET THAT FORM A SPECIFIC CHORD PATTERN. THERE ARE ALSO MORE THAN ONE FINGER PATTERN FOR THE SAME CHORD. THIS BOOK WILL PRESENT THE SIMPLEST AND MOST COMMONLY PLAYED PATTERNS.

"OPEN" CHORDS ARE CHORDS IN WHICH SOME STRINGS OF THE CHORD ARE NOT PRESSED DOWN WITH YOUR FINGERS, HOWEVER ALL THE STRINGS ARE PLAYED EXCEPT THOSE INDICATED BY A BROKEN LINE.

"BARRE" CHORDS ARE CHORDS IN WHICH ALL THE STRINGS OF THE CHORD ARE PRESSED DOWN WITH YOUR FINGERS AND ALL THE STRINGS ARE PLAYED EXCEPT THOSE INDICATED BY A BROKEN LINE.

"OPEN" & "BARRE"
CHORD COMBINATIONS

The following pages will consist of chord combinations in "Open" Form and located directly below will be the same chord combination in "Barre" Form. This gives you a choice as to whether you want to play a chord in "Open" Form or "Barre" Form. This will make it possible to play the same chord in two different finger patterns and positions on the guitar neck, offering two different tones.

We will begin by practicing the fingering positions of the four chord "Open" Chord Combination at the top of the following pages.

You may wish to wait a while before going on to practicing the "Barre" Chord Form Combinations as they require a little more practice in finger positioning.

You can play "Open" Chord Forms and "Barre" Chord Forms mixed together. Following the "Open" and "Barre" Form Chord Combinations will be some examples which we will refer to as the Mixed "Open" & "Barre" Form Combination pages.

REMEMBER TO USE THE CONSISTENT SUCCESSIVE ORDER OF NOTES IN THE CHROMATIC SCALE IN THE EVENT YOU WISH TO MOVE A CHORD UP OR DOWN THE GUITAR NECK, THE FIRST LETTER OF A CHORD NAME WILL FOLLOW THE SAME ORDER, FOR EXAMPLE, IF YOU, ARE PLAYING AN "F" MAJOR CHORD FINGER PATTERN AND WISH TO MOVE THE ENTIRE PATTERN ONE FRET TOWARD THE BODY OF THE GUITAR (BEING SURE TO KEEP YOUR FINGERS ON THE SAME STRINGS OR FINGER PATTERN) THE NEXT CHORD WOULD BE AN "F#" MAJOR CHORD, NEXT WOULD BE A "G" MAJOR CHORD AND SO FORTH.....

**ALL "BARRE" CHORDS ARE MOVABLE CHORDS.

**SEE "MOVABLE GUITAR CHORDS" BOX ON PAGE 40 TO BETTER UNDERSTAND WHICH "OPEN" CHORDS ARE MOVABLE CHORDS. IN THE FOLLOWING CHORD COMBINATIONS BEGINNING ON THE NEXT PAGE THAT ARE IN "OPEN" CHORD FORM, ONLY THE "F" CHORD IS A "MOVABLE CHORD."

RHYTHM: SLOWLY OR MODERATELY STRUM <u>EACH</u> CHORD YOU PLAY AT LEAST FOUR TIMES, TO A COUNT OF FOUR, TRY TAPPING YOUR FOOT TO KEEP COUNT (1 ANNA 2 ANNA 3 ANNA 4), OR UNTIL YOU FIND WHAT IS COMFORTABLE FOR YOU. (THE "NUMBER" COUNT IS WHEN YOUR FOOT TAPS THE FLOOR, THE "ANNA" COUNT IS WHEN YOUR FOOT IS RAISED).

CHORD COMBINATION IN "OPEN" CHORD FORM

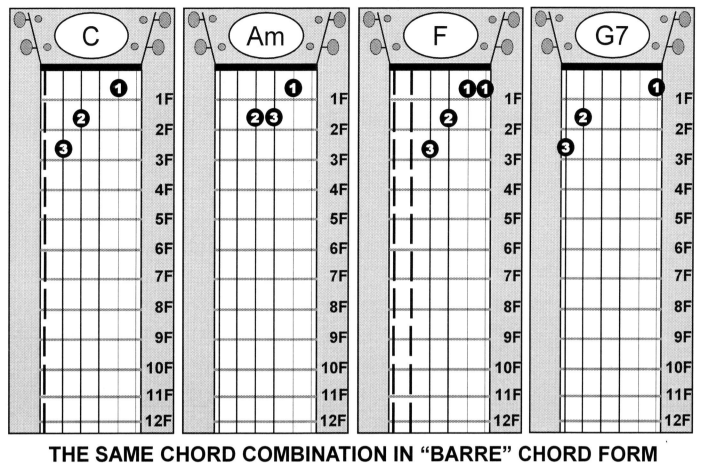

THE SAME CHORD COMBINATION IN "BARRE" CHORD FORM

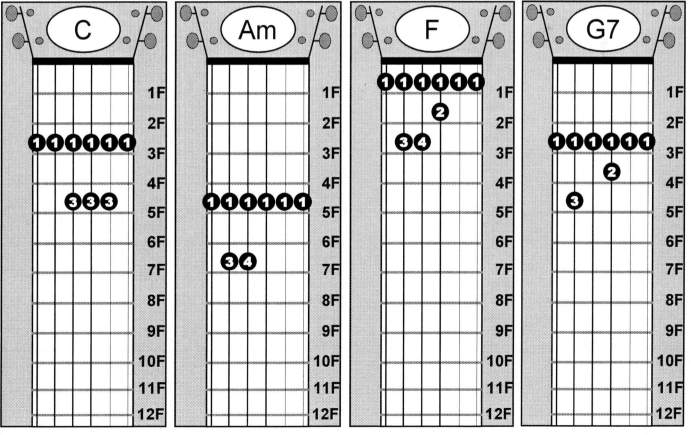

CHORD COMBINATION IN "OPEN" CHORD FORM

THE SAME CHORD COMBINATION IN "BARRE" CHORD FORM

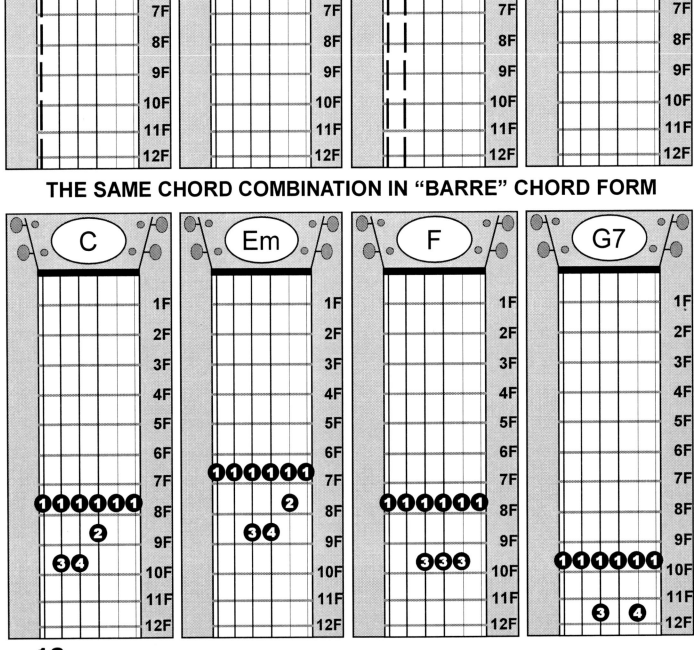

CHORD COMBINATION IN "OPEN" CHORD FORM

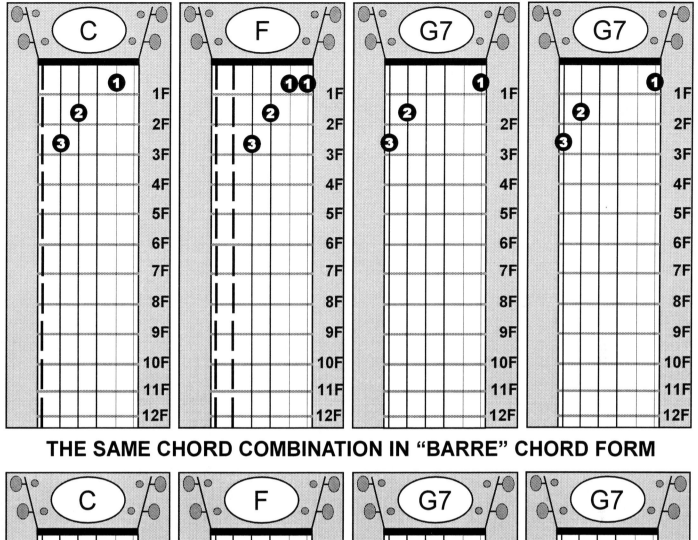

THE SAME CHORD COMBINATION IN "BARRE" CHORD FORM

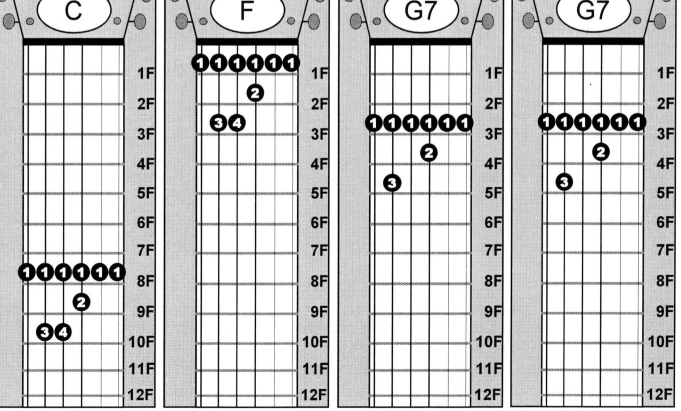

CHORD COMBINATION IN "OPEN" CHORD FORM

THE SAME CHORD COMBINATION IN "BARRE" CHORD FORM

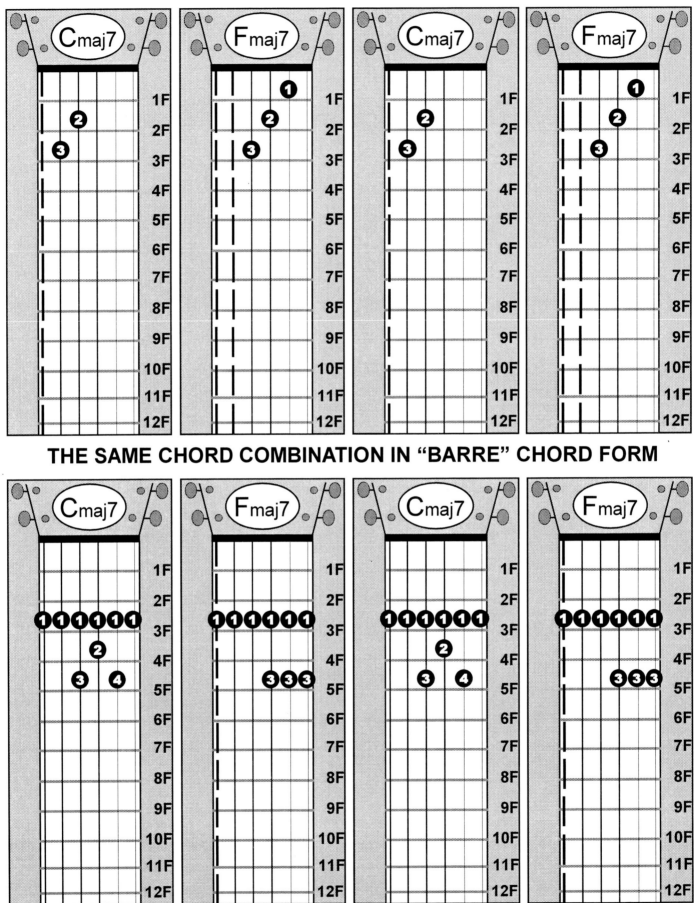

20

CHORD COMBINATION IN "OPEN" CHORD FORM

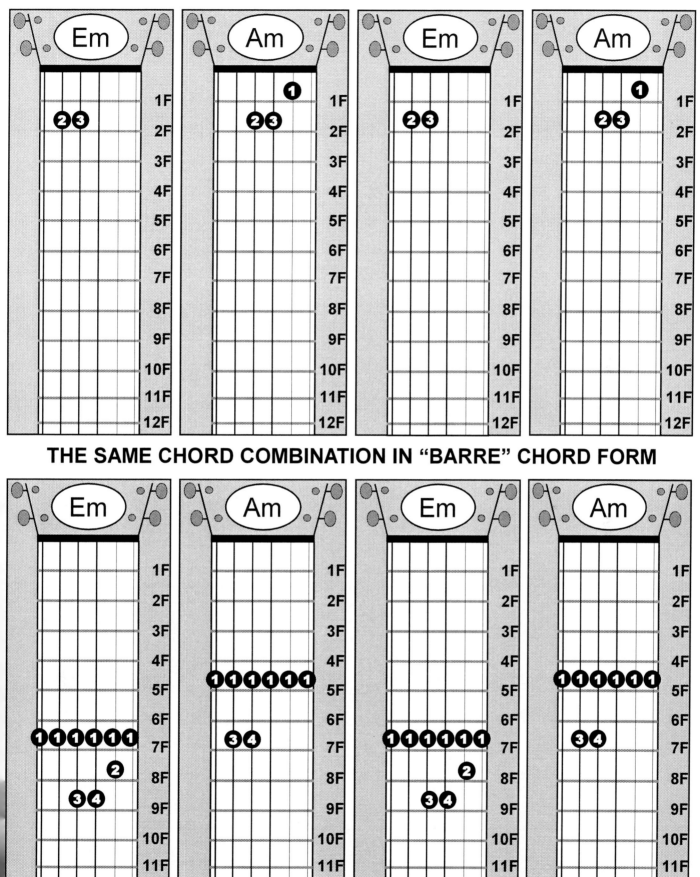

THE SAME CHORD COMBINATION IN "BARRE" CHORD FORM

CHORD COMBINATION IN "OPEN" CHORD FORM

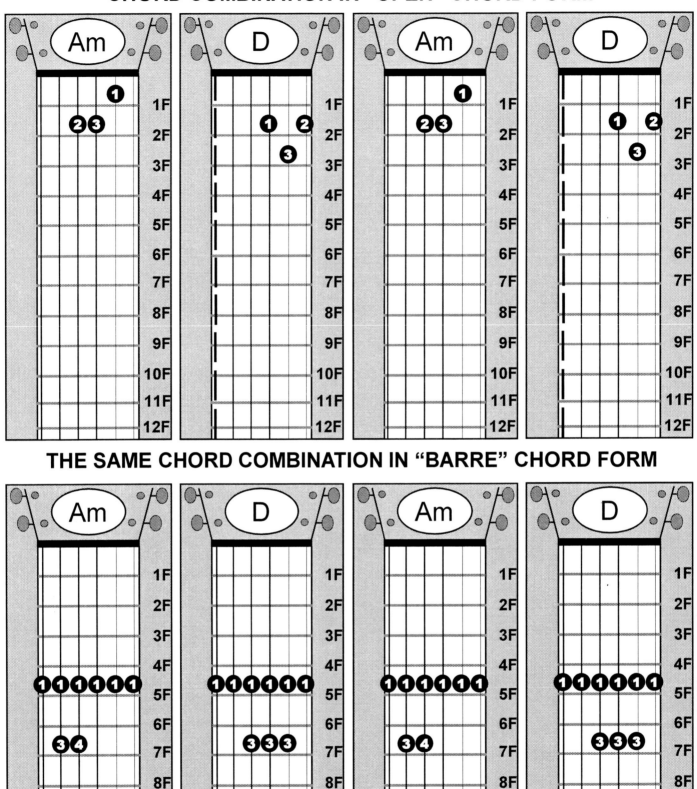

THE SAME CHORD COMBINATION IN "BARRE" CHORD FORM

22

CHORD COMBINATION IN "OPEN" CHORD FORM

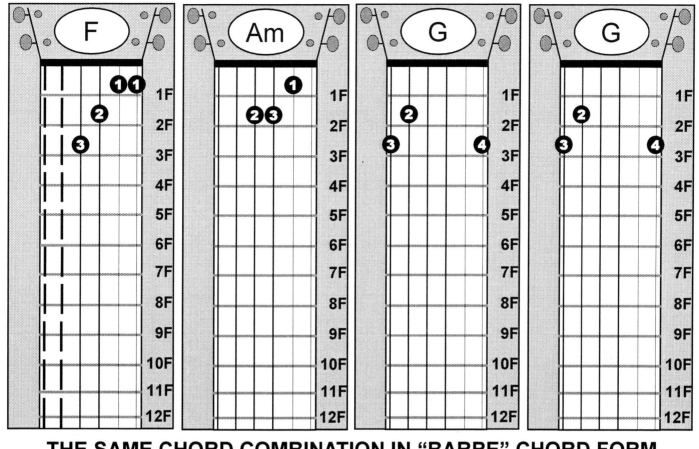

THE SAME CHORD COMBINATION IN "BARRE" CHORD FORM

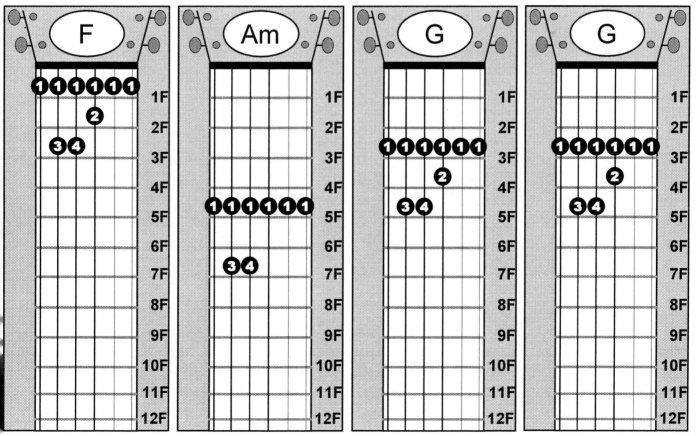

CHORD COMBINATION IN "OPEN" CHORD FORM

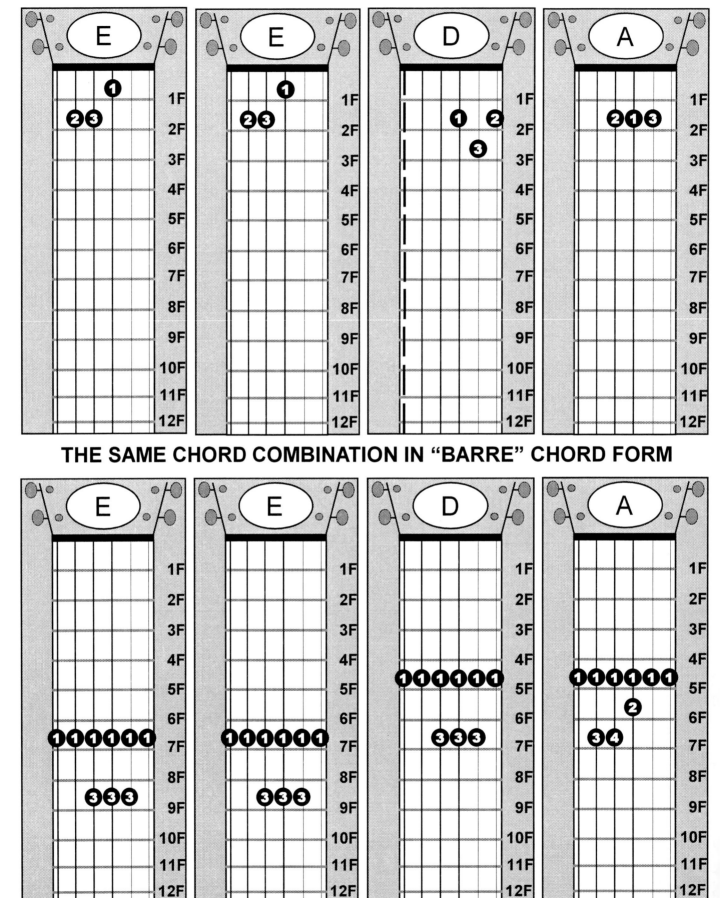

THE SAME CHORD COMBINATION IN "BARRE" CHORD FORM

CHORD COMBINATION IN "OPEN" CHORD FORM

THE SAME CHORD COMBINATION IN "BARRE" CHORD FORM

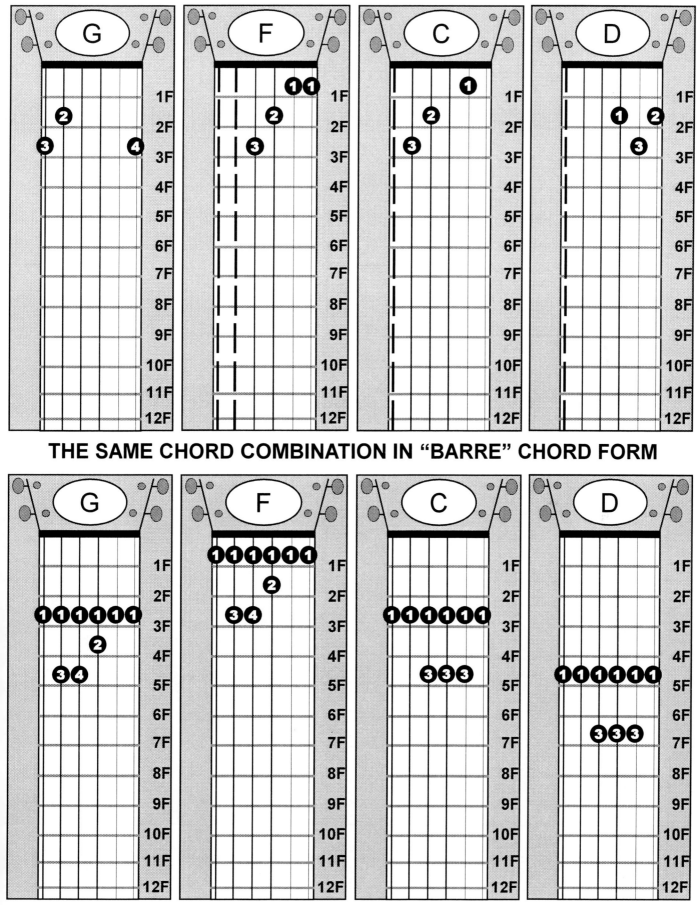

25

CHORD COMBINATION IN "OPEN" CHORD FORM

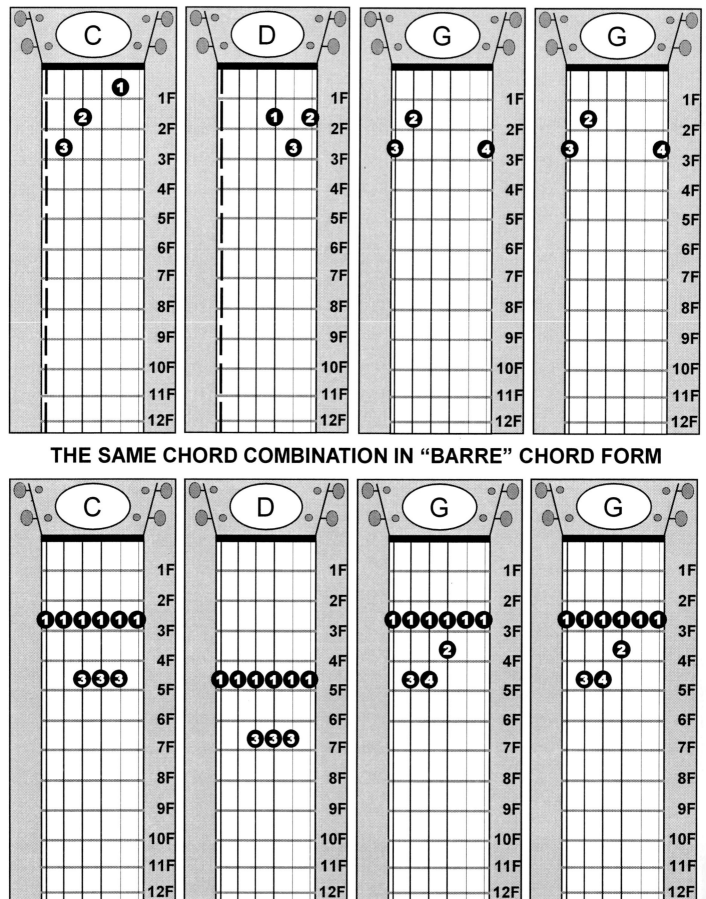

THE SAME CHORD COMBINATION IN "BARRE" CHORD FORM

26

CHORD COMBINATION IN "OPEN" CHORD FORM

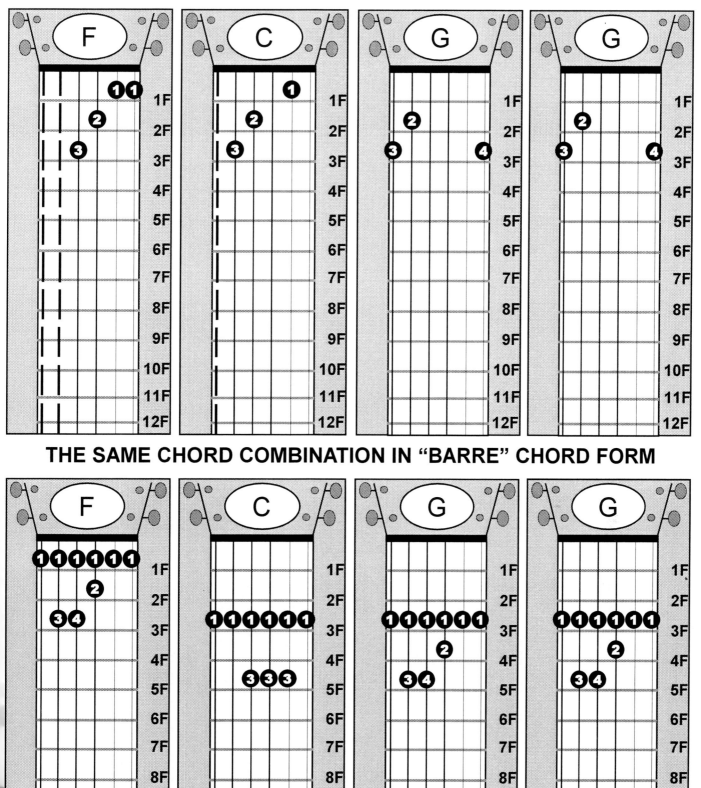

THE SAME CHORD COMBINATION IN "BARRE" CHORD FORM

INSTANT CHORD CHANGES

As you become more familiar with positioning your fingers to form "Barre" chords, you will discover that you can make two or four different forms of chords from just one chord.

It is easy as lifting one or more fingers. In the chord diagrams below, we begin with one of the most commonly used finger pattern forms for the Major Chords, in this case, the "F" Major Chord. By lifting the gray colored number 2 finger (Middle Finger) you will create an "F" Minor Chord, then by lifting the gray colored number 2 and 4 finger (Middle and Pinky Finger) you will create an "F" Minor Seventh Chord and finally by lifting the number 4 finger (Pinky Finger) you will create an "F" Dominant Seventh Chord.

You can now move the entire "F" Major Chord finger pattern toward the body of the guitar to the next fret and you will be able to do the same with the next chord which will be an "F#" Major Chord. You can continue doing this up and down the guitar neck forming more and more chords.

*Below the F7 Chord is another form of the F7 Chord. Playing the bottom F7 Chord form adds a higher pitch to the chord. The choice is yours on deciding the form you desire.

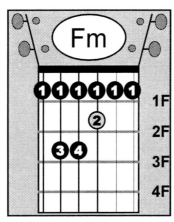
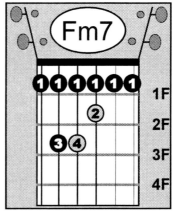
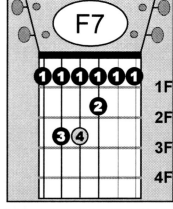
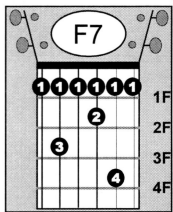

INSTANT CHORD CHANGES

In the first two diagrams below you can instantly change a "Cm" Chord into a "Cm7" Chord by lifting just one finger. When you lift the gray colored number 4 finger (Pinky Finger) off the "Cm" Chord you will create a "Cm7" Chord as illustrated in the second diagram.

In the second two diagrams below you can instantly change a "Cmaj7" Chord into a "C7" Chord by lifting just one finger. When you lift the gray colored number 2 finger (Middle Finger) off the "Cmaj7" Chord you will create a "C7" Chord as illustrated in the fourth diagram.

*Below the Cm7 Chord is another form of the Cm7 Chord. Playing the bottom Cm7 Chord form adds a higher pitch to the chord. The choice is yours on deciding the form you desire.

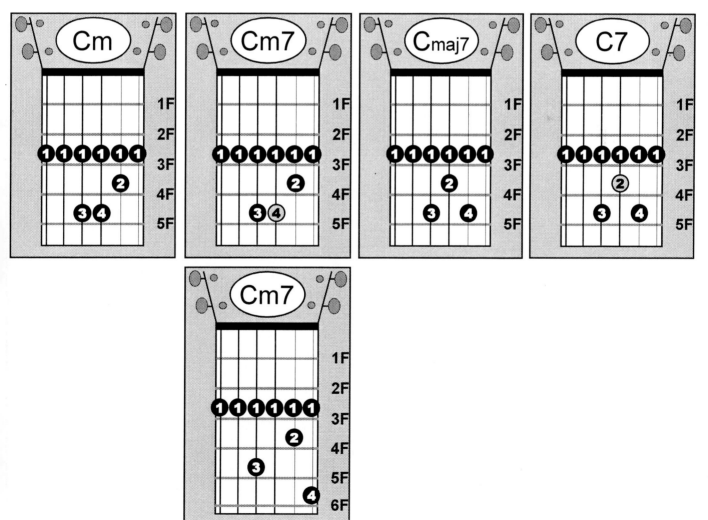

"BARRE" CHORD FINGER POSITIONING

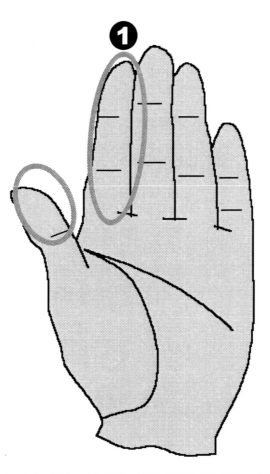

* WHEN PLAYING "BARRE CHORDS" USE THE ENTIRE INDEX FINGER (NUMBER 1 FINGER) TO HOLD THE STRINGS FIRMLY DOWN WHERE INDICATED ON CHORD DIAGRAMS.

* YOU CAN ALSO USE EITHER OF THE TWO FORMS OF FINGERING BELOW FOR PLAYING THE SECOND PORTION OF A "BARRE" CHORD:

* ONLY THE UPPER PORTION OF THE THUMB WILL REST ON THE BACK NECK OF GUITAR.

"BARRE" CHORDS

A "BARRE CHORD" (Pronounced Bar) IS WHEN THE INDEX FINGER IS PLACED ACROSS ALL THE STRINGS ALONG SIDE OF A FRET. THIS WILL ALLOW YOU TO PLAY ANOTHER FINGER FORM OF THE SAME CHORD YOU PREVIOUSLY PLAYED AS AN OPEN CHORD, THEREBY PRODUCING A COMPLETELY NEW SOUND TO THE CHORD. MANY OF THE CHORDS YOU LEARNED EARLIER CAN BE PLAYED BY USING A FINGER FORM "BARRE CHORD," ALLOWING YOU TO PLAY THE SAME CHORD BUT IN A DIFFERENT FINGER FORM AND LOCATION ON THE GUITAR NECK.

THE FOLLOWING ARE "BARRE CHORDS." THE NUMBER 2, 3, OR 4 FINGER WILL MAINTAIN THE ORIGINAL CHORD FINGER PATTERN YOU PREVIOUSLY LEARNED, HOWEVER, AS THE ORIGINAL CHORD FINGER PATTERN MOVES ONE NOTE AND FRET DOWN TOWARD THE BODY OF THE GUITAR, THE INDEX FINGER TAKES ON A BARRE POSITION AND A NEW CHORD IS MADE. THE SEQUENCE CHORDS WILL FOLLOW EACH OTHER IN NAME IN THE SAME ORDER AS IN THE CHROMATIC SCALE OF NOTES:
E, F, (F# also called G♭), G, (G# also called A♭), A, (A# also called B♭), B, C, (C# also called D♭), D, (D# also called E♭).

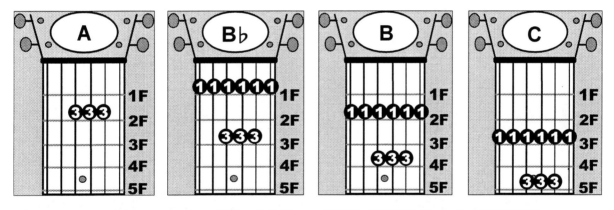

*   THE NEXT CHORD THAT WILL FOLLOW THE "C" CHORD IN THIS BARRE CHORD FINGER
     PATTERN WILL BE THE "C#" CHORD, THEN THE "D" CHORD, AND SO FORTH.................

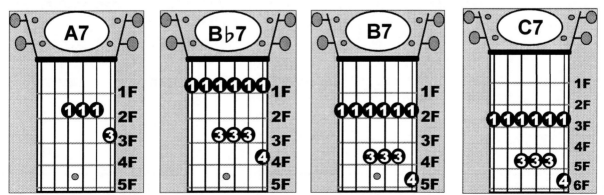

*   THE NEXT CHORD THAT WILL FOLLOW THE "C7" CHORD IN THIS BARRE CHORD FINGER
     PATTERN WILL BE THE "C#7" CHORD, THEN THE "D7" CHORD, AND SO FORTH.................

"BARRE" CHORDS

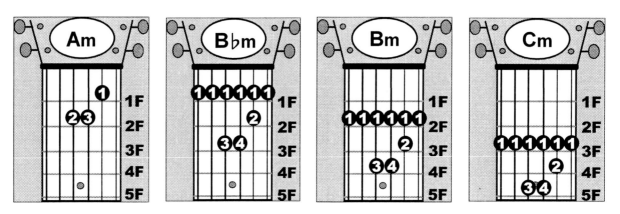

*   THE NEXT CHORD THAT WILL FOLLOW THE "Cm" CHORD IN THIS BARRE CHORD FINGER
    PATTERN WILL BE THE "C#m" CHORD, THEN THE "Dm" CHORD, AND SO FORTH.................

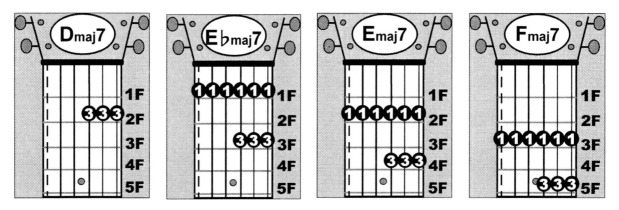

*   THE NEXT CHORD THAT WILL FOLLOW THE "Fmaj7" CHORD IN THIS BARRE CHORD FINGER
    PATTERN WILL BE THE "F#maj7" CHORD, THEN THE "Gmaj7" CHORD, AND SO FORTH.................

"BARRE" CHORDS

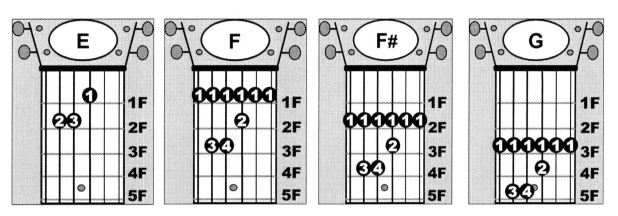

* THE NEXT CHORD THAT WILL FOLLOW THE "G" CHORD IN THIS BARRE CHORD FINGER
PATTERN WILL BE THE "G#" CHORD, THEN THE "A" CHORD, AND SO FORTH.................

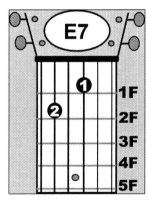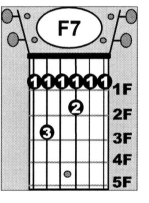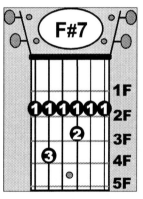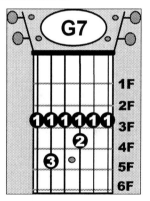

* THE NEXT CHORD THAT WILL FOLLOW THE "G7" CHORD IN THIS BARRE CHORD FINGER
PATTERN WILL BE THE "G#7" CHORD, THEN THE "A7" CHORD, AND SO FORTH.................

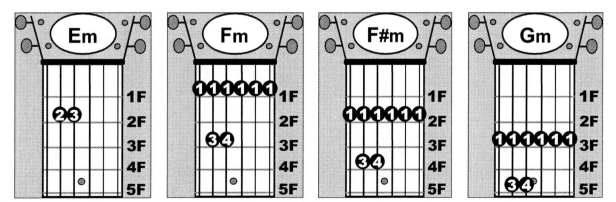

* THE NEXT CHORD THAT WILL FOLLOW THE "Gm" CHORD IN THIS BARRE CHORD FINGER
PATTERN WILL BE THE "G#m" CHORD, THEN THE "Am" CHORD, AND SO FORTH.................

MIXED "OPEN" & "BARRE" CHORD COMBINATIONS

BELOW ARE 5 SEPARATE CHORD GROUPS, "BARRE" CHORDS MIXED WITH "OPEN" CHORDS. NOW YOU HAVE A CHOICE OF PLAYING A BARRE CHORD OR PLAYING AN "OPEN" CHORD FINGER PATTERN. REMEMBER YOU CAN PRODUCE SOME OF YOUR OWN CHORD COMBINATIONS IN EITHER A BARRE FORM AND/OR WITH AN OPEN FORM FINGER PATTERN, JUST USE THE CHORD COMBINATION DIAGRAM ON PAGE 56, THERE ARE MANY TO CREATE.

SLOWLY OR MODERATELY STRUM <u>EACH</u> CHORD YOU PLAY AT LEAST FOUR TIMES, TO A COUNT OF FOUR, TRY TAPPING YOUR FOOT TO KEEP COUNT (1 ANNA 2 ANNA 3 ANNA 4), OR UNTIL YOU FIND WHAT IS COMFORTABLE FOR YOU. (THE "NUMBER" COUNT IS WHEN YOUR FOOT TAPS THE FLOOR, THE "ANNA" COUNT IS WHEN YOUR FOOT IS RAISED).

1ST CHORD GROUP

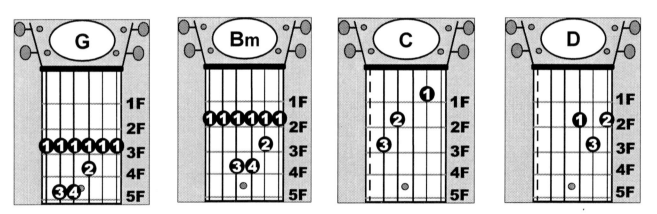

2ND CHORD GROUP

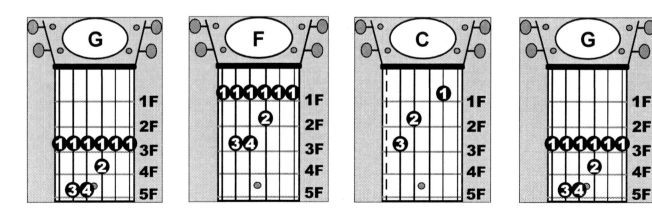

34

3RD CHORD GROUP

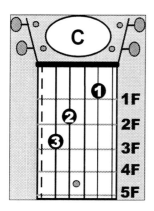
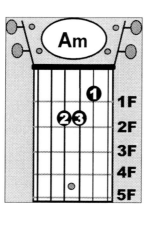
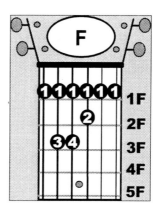
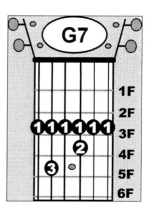

4TH CHORD GROUP

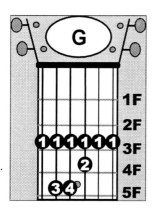
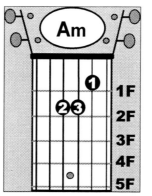
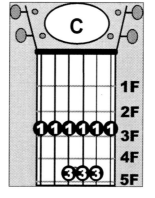
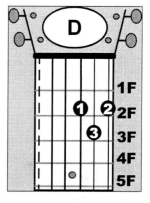

5TH CHORD GROUP

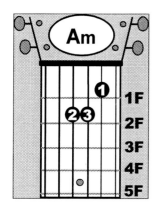
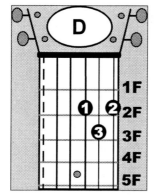
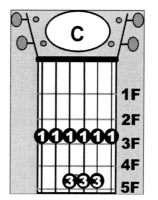
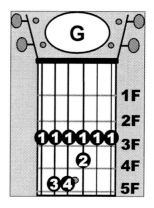

TRANSPOSING CHORD PATTERNS

SOMETIMES A MELODY OR SONG MAY BE TOO HIGH OR TOO LOW FOR YOUR VOICE. YOU CAN CHANGE ANY CHORD PATTERN TO A HIGHER OR LOWER CHORD PATTERN TO SUIT YOUR VOICE.

<u>REMEMBER THAT THE FIRST LETTER OF THE FIRST CHORD ALWAYS DETERMINES WHERE THE ORDER OF A CHORD PATTERN BEGINS</u>.

WHEN YOU CHANGE A CHORD PATTERN, REMEMBER THAT YOU WILL ONLY NEED TO CHANGE THE FIRST LETTER OF EACH CHORD, ALL OTHER NOTATIONS IN EACH CHORD REMAIN THE SAME AND CARRY OVER TO THE NEW CHORD PATTERN, (These Are Called "Extensions," The Extension of "Am" is the "m," The Extension of "Amaj7" is the "maj7" and so forth).   FOR EXAMPLE, CHANGING ANY "A" CHORDS TO "G" CHORDS:

Am BECOMES Gm

Amaj7 BECOMES Gmaj7

A7 BECOMES G7

A9 BECOMES G9

IN ORDER FOR YOU TO UNDERSTAND HOW TO TRANSPOSE CHORD PATTERNS, THREE ORIGINAL CHORD PATTERNS HAVE BEEN MAPPED OUT FOR YOU ON THE STRING NOTE DIAGRAM ON PAGES 37, 38 AND 39.

(USE ONLY TOP FOUR STRINGS TO MAP OUT CHORD PATTERNS)

ON PAGE 37, THE ORIGINAL CHORD PATTERN BEGINS WITH A "C Major" CHORD, THEN GOES TO AN "Am" CHORD, THEN TO A "F Major" CHORD, AND FINALLY TO A "G7" CHORD. NOTICE ON THE STRING NOTE DIAGRAM THAT THE "A" NOTE (WHICH REPRESENTS THE "Am" CHORD) IS THREE FRETS AWAY FROM THE "C" NOTE AND THE "F" NOTE IS DIRECTLY BELOW THE "C" NOTE AND THE "G" NOTE IS TWO FRETS AWAY FROM THE "F" NOTE.

NOW WE WILL TRANSPOSE THE CHORD PATTERN TO BEGIN WITH AN "A Major" CHORD, SINCE THE "A Major" WAS CHOSEN AS THE <u>FIRST CHORD</u>, THE REMAINDER OF THE NEW CHORD PATTERN WILL BE "F#m", "D Major", AND "E Major." (AS SHOWN IN THE STRING NOTE DIAGRAM ON PAGE 37)

36

*TRANSPOSING CHORD PATTERNS

YOU WILL SEE BELOW AND ON THE FOLLOWING PAGES THAT THE TRANSPOSED CHORD PATTERNS FOLLOW EXACTLY THE SAME PATTERNS AS THE ORIGINAL CHORD PATTERNS.

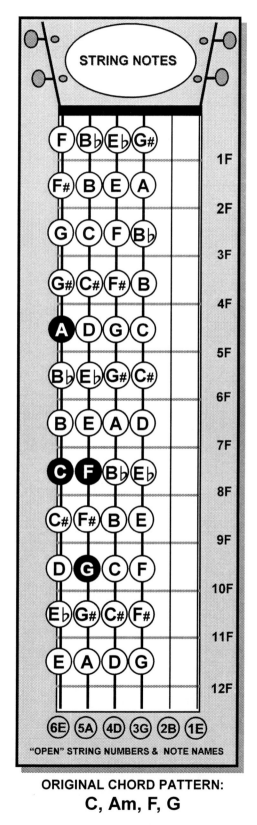

ORIGINAL CHORD PATTERN:
C, Am, F, G

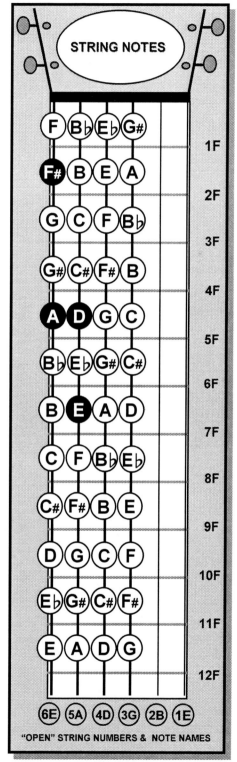

TRANSPOSED TO BEGIN WITH AN "A" CHORD:
A, F#m, D, E

*TRANSPOSING CHORD PATTERNS

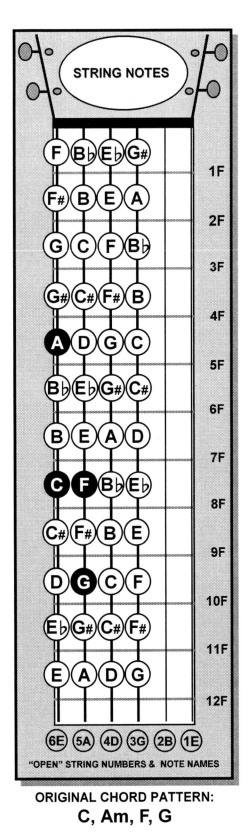

ORIGINAL CHORD PATTERN:
C, Am, F, G

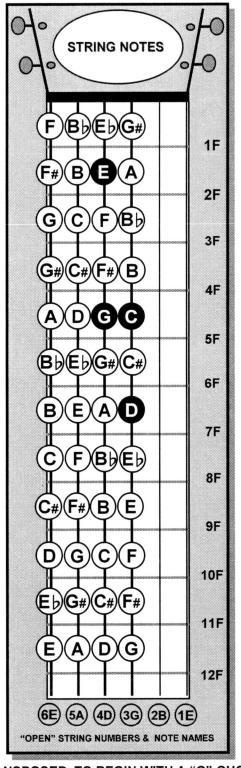

TRANSPOSED TO BEGIN WITH A "G" CHORD:
G, Em, C, D

*TRANSPOSING CHORD PATTERNS

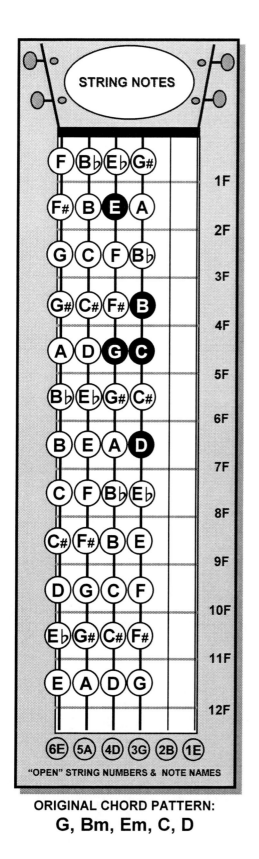

ORIGINAL CHORD PATTERN:
G, Bm, Em, C, D

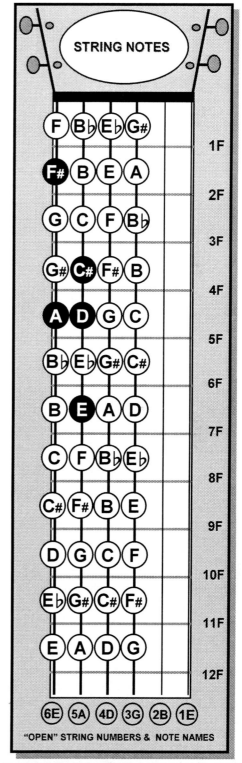

TRANSPOSED TO BEGIN WITH AN "A" CHORD:
A, C#m, F#m, D, E

39

HOW TO READ "OPEN" CHORD DIAGRAMS

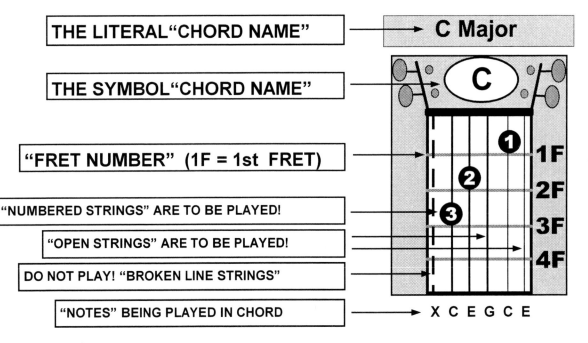

THE LITERAL"CHORD NAME" → C Major

THE SYMBOL"CHORD NAME"

"FRET NUMBER" (1F = 1st FRET)

"NUMBERED STRINGS" ARE TO BE PLAYED!

"OPEN STRINGS" ARE TO BE PLAYED!

DO NOT PLAY! "BROKEN LINE STRINGS"

"NOTES" BEING PLAYED IN CHORD → X C E G C E

* BE SURE YOUR FINGERS ARE PLACED ON THE PROPER FRET POSITION.
(FRETS HAVE BEEN NUMBERED TO HELP IN POSITIONING OF FINGERS).

* BE SURE TO PLACE NUMBERED FINGERS NEAR THE FRETS
(AS SHOWN IN CHORD DIAGRAMS).

* THE GUITAR CHORDS ARE IDENTIFIED WITH TWO NAMES, THE FIRST IS THE LITERAL NAME
OF THE CHORD, THE SAME CHORD CAN ALSO BE IDENTIFIED BY A LETTER OR WITH A
LETTER AND A NUMBER (SYMBOL NAME) AS IS OFTEN THE CASE IN SHEET MUSIC.

MOVABLE GUITAR CHORDS

IF A CHORD HAS NO "OPEN STRINGS" (THIS DOES NOT INCLUDE THE BROKEN LINE STRINGS),
THAT CHORD CAN BE MOVED UP AND DOWN THE NECK OF THE GUITAR. BE SURE TO KEEP THE
ORIGINAL CHORD FINGERING POSITIONS OF THE CHORD YOU CHOOSE TO MOVE. FOR
EXAMPLE, THE "Cm" CHORD WILL BECOME A "C#m" CHORD BY MOVING THE NUMBER 1 FINGER
POSITIONS (INDEX FINGER) TO THE 4TH FRET, THE NUMBER 2 FINGER POSITION
(MIDDLE FINGER) TO THE 5TH FRET AND THE NUMBER 3 FINGER POSITION (RING FINGER) TO
THE 6TH FRET AND THE NUMBER 4 FINGER POSITION (PINKY FINGER) TO THE 6TH FRET.

THE FIRST LETTER CHORD NAMES WILL FOLLOW EACH OTHER IN THE SAME ORDER AS IN THE
SCALE OF NOTES: E, F, (F# also called Gb), G, (G# also called Ab), A, (A# also called Bb), B, C,
(C# also called Db), D, (D# also called Eb). TO BETTER UNDERSTAND, LOOK AT THE "GUITAR
STRING NOTE NAMES" DIAGRAM ON PAGE 10 AND NOTICE THE ORDER IN WHICH THE NOTES
FOLLOW EACH OTHER. THE F#, FOLLOWS THE F NOTE, THEN THE G NOTE FOLLOWS THE F#
NOTE. THE SAME WOULD BE TRUE OF CHORDS. ANOTHER EXAMPLE, THE "F#m" (MINOR) CHORD
WOULD BECOME A "Gm" (MINOR) CHORD WHEN MOVING THIS PARTICULAR CHORD FINGERING
POSITION TOWARD THE BODY OF THE GUITAR ONE FRET, THE NEXT CHORD WOULD BE A
"G#m" (MINOR) CHORD AND SO FORTH.

"C" Chords

C Major

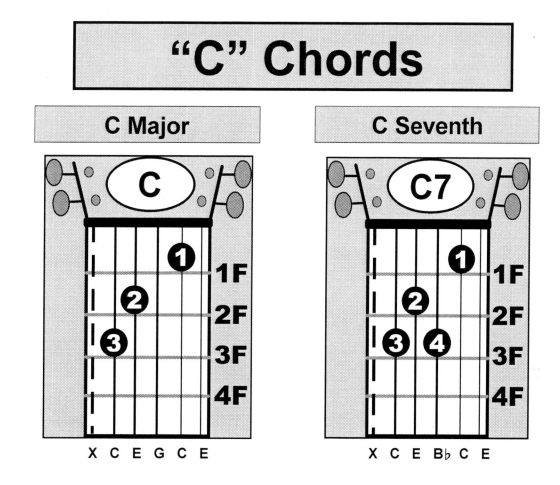

C Seventh

* PLAY ALL STRINGS: NUMBERED FINGER STRINGS AND "OPEN STRINGS"
HOWEVER, DO NOT PLAY "BROKEN LINE STRINGS"

C Minor

*"Cm"
Is A
Movable
Chord

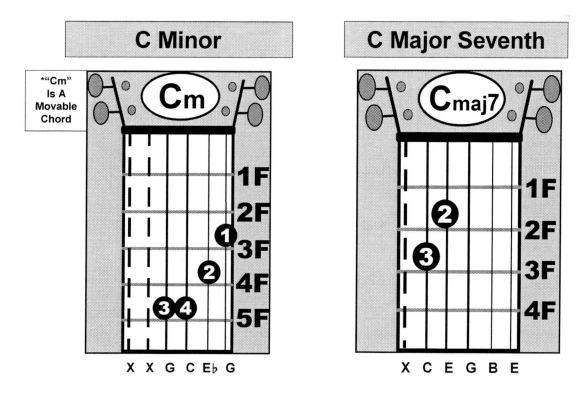

C Major Seventh

*TIPS ALONG THE WAY

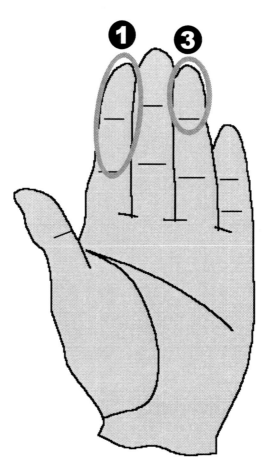

* WHEN MORE THAN ONE STRING MUST BE HELD DOWN WITH THE INDEX FINGER (NUMBER 1 FINGER) AT THE SAME TIME, PLACE AS MUCH AS NECESSARY OF CIRCLED PORTION OF INDEX FINGER FIRMLY DOWN OVER ALL THE STRINGS WHICH ARE GROUPED TOGETHER WITH THE NUMBERS 1.

* WHEN MORE THAN ONE STRING MUST BE HELD DOWN WITH THE RING FINGER (NUMBER 3 FINGER) AT THE SAME TIME, PLACE AS MUCH AS NECESSARY OF CIRCLED PORTION OF RING FINGER FIRMLY DOWN OVER ALL THE STRINGS WHICH ARE GROUPED TOGETHER WITH THE NUMBERS 3.

TIP: PRESS THE TIP OF YOUR RING FINGER AGAINST THE TIP OF YOUR THUMB, NOTICE THAT YOUR RING FINGER SLIGHTLY ARCHES, THIS WILL HELP IN POSITIONING YOUR FINGER OVER THE THREE STRINGS. YOU CAN ALSO PLAY THE OPENED "A" CHORD WITH THE NUMBER 3 FINGER AS SHOWN HERE:

"A" Chords

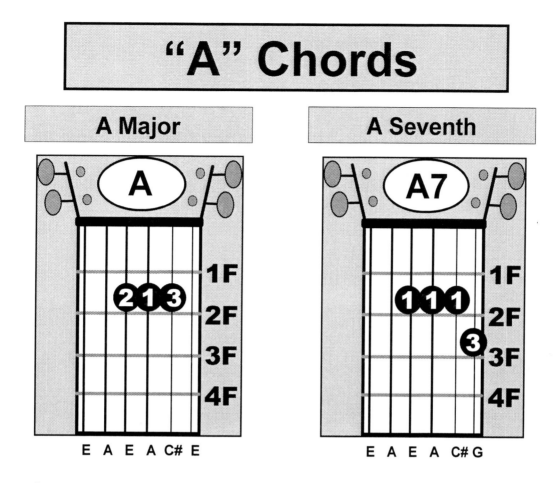

A Major

A

1F
②①③
2F
3F
4F

E A E A C# E

A Seventh

A7

1F
①①①
2F
③
3F
4F

E A E A C# G

* PLAY ALL STRINGS: NUMBERED FINGER STRINGS AND "OPEN STRINGS"
HOWEVER, DO NOT PLAY "BROKEN LINE STRINGS"

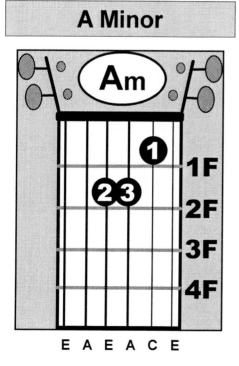

A Minor

Am

①
1F
②③
2F
3F
4F

E A E A C E

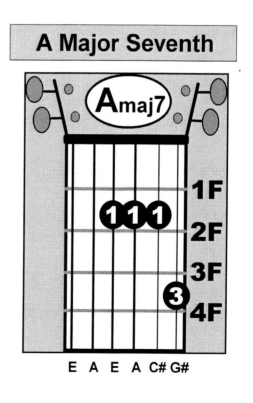

A Major Seventh

Amaj7

1F
①①①
2F
3F
③
4F

E A E A C# G#

43

"F" Chords

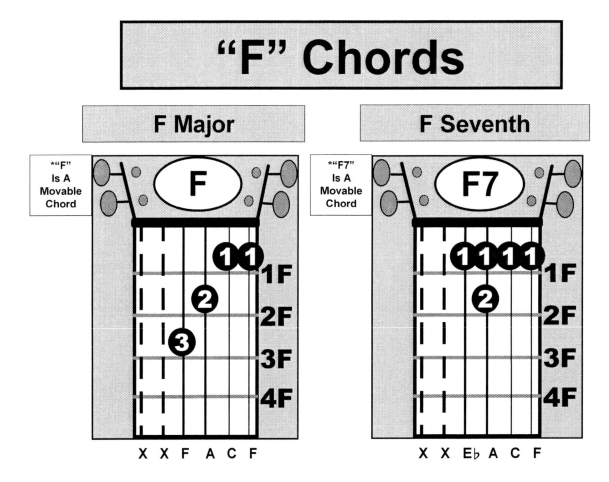

F Major

*"F" Is A Movable Chord

F

1F
2F
3F
4F

X X F A C F

F Seventh

*"F7" Is A Movable Chord

F7

1F
2F
3F
4F

X X E♭ A C F

* PLAY ALL STRINGS: NUMBERED FINGER STRINGS AND "OPEN STRINGS"
HOWEVER, DO NOT PLAY "BROKEN LINE STRINGS"

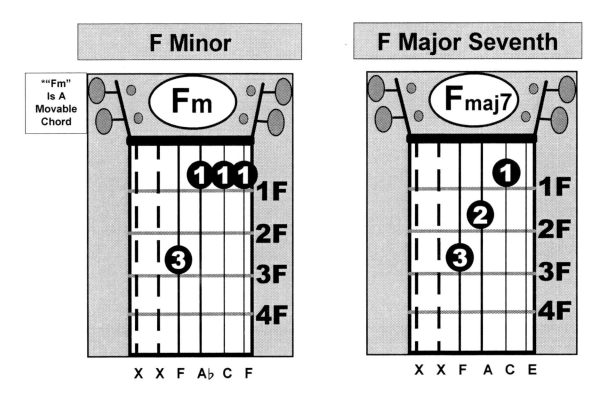

F Minor

*"Fm" Is A Movable Chord

Fm

1F
2F
3F
4F

X X F A♭ C F

F Major Seventh

Fmaj7

1F
2F
3F
4F

X X F A C E

44

"G" Chords

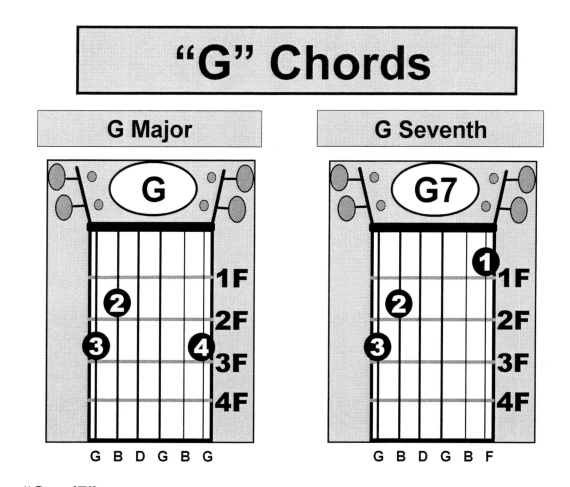

G Major

G

1F
2
2F
3   4
3F
4F

G B D G B G

G Seventh

G7

1
1F
2
2F
3
3F
4F

G B D G B F

---

*   **"Gmaj7":**   USE THE NUMBER 3 FINGER OF THE LEFT HAND TO MUFFLE THE 5TH
STRING BY SLIGHTLY FLATTENING THE FIRST FINGER JOINT WHILE LIGHTLY TOUCHING
THE 5TH STRING.

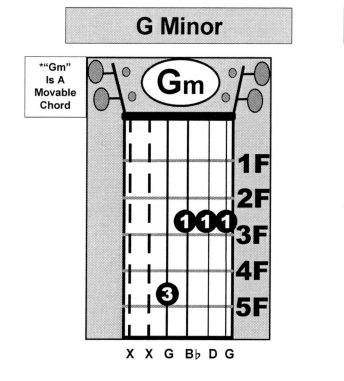

G Minor

*"Gm"
Is A
Movable
Chord

Gm

1F
2F
1 1 1
3F
4F
3
5F

X X G B♭ D G

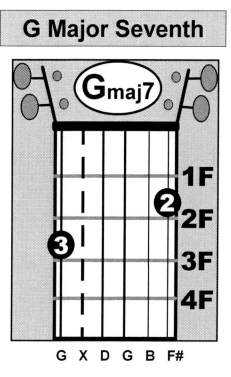

G Major Seventh

Gmaj7

1F
2
2F
3
3F
4F

G X D G B F#

45

"D" Chords

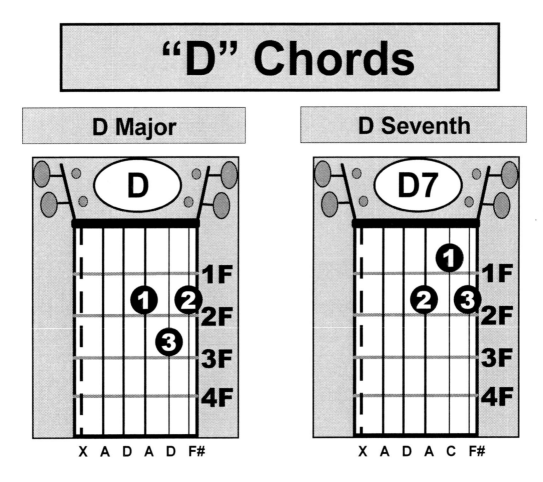

D Major

D

1F
1 2 — 2F
3 — 3F
4F

X A D A D F#

D Seventh

D7

1 — 1F
2 3 — 2F
3F
4F

X A D A C F#

* PLAY ALL STRINGS: NUMBERED FINGER STRINGS AND "OPEN STRINGS"
HOWEVER, DO NOT PLAY "BROKEN LINE STRINGS"

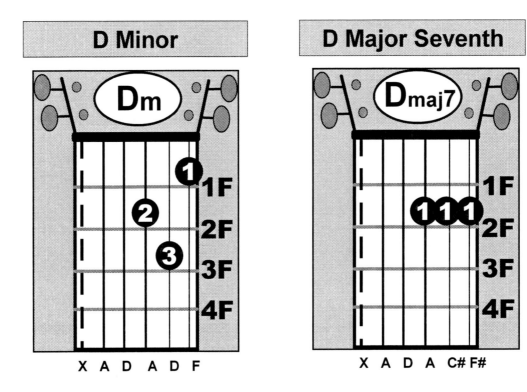

D Minor

Dm

1 — 1F
2 — 2F
3 — 3F
4F

X A D A D F

D Major Seventh

Dmaj7

1F
1 1 1 — 2F
3F
4F

X A D A C# F#

"E" Chords

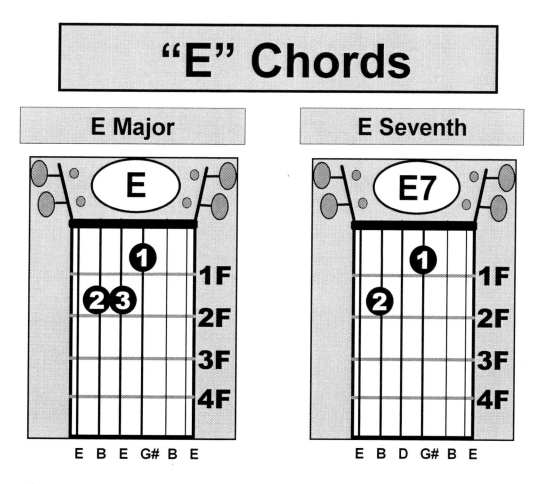

E Major

E

1F
2F
3F
4F

E B E G# B E

E Seventh

E7

1F
2F
3F
4F

E B D G# B E

* PLAY ALL STRINGS: NUMBERED FINGER STRINGS AND "OPEN STRINGS"
HOWEVER, DO NOT PLAY "BROKEN LINE STRINGS"

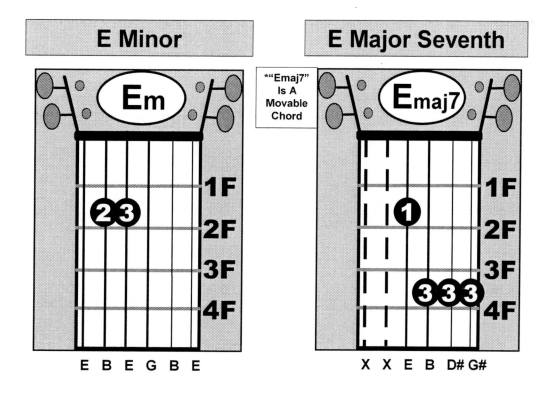

E Minor

Em

1F
2F
3F
4F

E B E G B E

*"Emaj7"
Is A
Movable
Chord

E Major Seventh

Emaj7

1F
2F
3F
4F

X X E B D# G#

"B" Chords

B Major

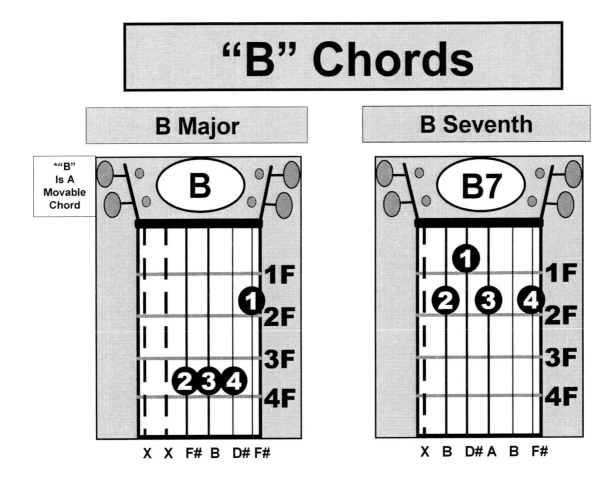

*"B" Is A Movable Chord

B

1F
1
2F

3F
2 3 4
4F

X X F# B D# F#

B Seventh

B7

1F
1
2 3 4
2F

3F

4F

X B D# A B F#

* PLAY ALL STRINGS: NUMBERED FINGER STRINGS AND "OPEN STRINGS"
HOWEVER, DO NOT PLAY "BROKEN LINE STRINGS"

B Minor

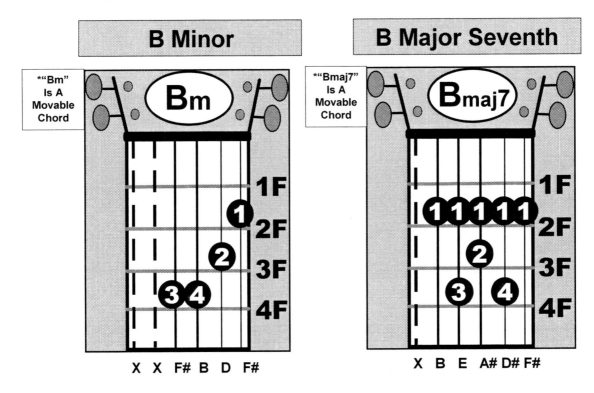

*"Bm" Is A Movable Chord

Bm

1F
1
2F

2
3F
3 4
4F

X X F# B D F#

B Major Seventh

*"Bmaj7" Is A Movable Chord

Bmaj7

1F
1 1 1 1
2F

2
3F
3   4
4F

X B E A# D# F#

48

* THE FOLLOWING PAGES WILL ILLUSTRATE THE SHARP (#) AND FLAT (♭) CHORDS.

* REMEMBER SHARP (#) AND FLAT (♭) CHORDS HAVE TWO DIFFERENT NAMES.

* PRACTICE AND PATIENCE ARE THE KEYS TO SUCCESSFULLY LEARNING TO PLAY THE GUITAR.

*TIPS ALONG THE WAY

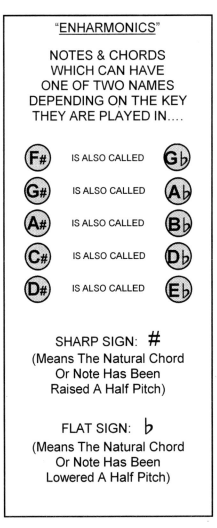

"ENHARMONICS"

NOTES & CHORDS
WHICH CAN HAVE
ONE OF TWO NAMES
DEPENDING ON THE KEY
THEY ARE PLAYED IN....

F#   IS ALSO CALLED   G♭

G#   IS ALSO CALLED   A♭

A#   IS ALSO CALLED   B♭

C#   IS ALSO CALLED   D♭

D#   IS ALSO CALLED   E♭

SHARP SIGN: #
(Means The Natural Chord
Or Note Has Been
Raised A Half Pitch)

FLAT SIGN: ♭
(Means The Natural Chord
Or Note Has Been
Lowered A Half Pitch)

* ABOVE IS AN ILLUSTRATION OF THE CHORDS AND NOTES WHICH HAVE TWO NAMES AND ALSO HAVE THE SAME FINGERING POSITIONS. FOR EXAMPLE, THE F# CHORD HAS THE SAME FINGERING AS THE G♭ CHORD. THE F#m CHORD HAS THE SAME FINGERING AS THE G♭m CHORD. THE B♭maj7 CHORD HAS THE SAME FINGERING AS THE A#maj7 CHORD. THE C#9 CHORD HAS THE SAME FINGERING AS THE D♭9 CHORD AND SO ON.

* **REMEMBER THAT THE FINGERING POSITIONS ARE THE SAME.**

"F#" Chords

F# Major

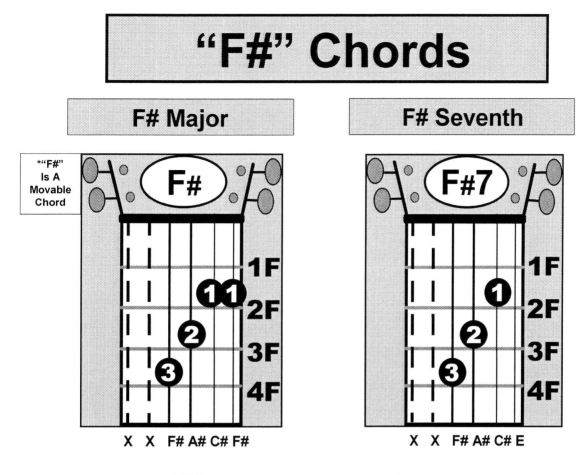

F#

1F
1 1 2F
2 3F
3 4F

X   X   F# A# C# F#

* F# CHORDS ARE ALSO CALLED Gb CHORDS

F# Seventh

F#7

1F
1 2F
2 3F
3 4F

X   X   F# A# C# E

F# Minor

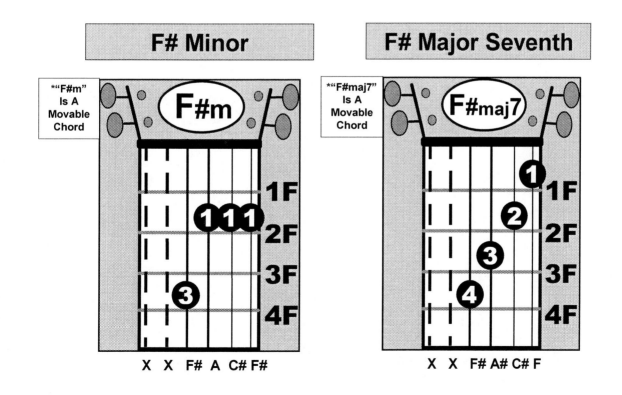

F#m

1F
1 1 1 2F
3F
3 4F

X   X   F# A   C# F#

F# Major Seventh

F#maj7

1
1F
2
2F
3
3F
4
4F

X   X   F# A# C# F

"G#" Chords

G# Major

*"G#" Is A Movable Chord

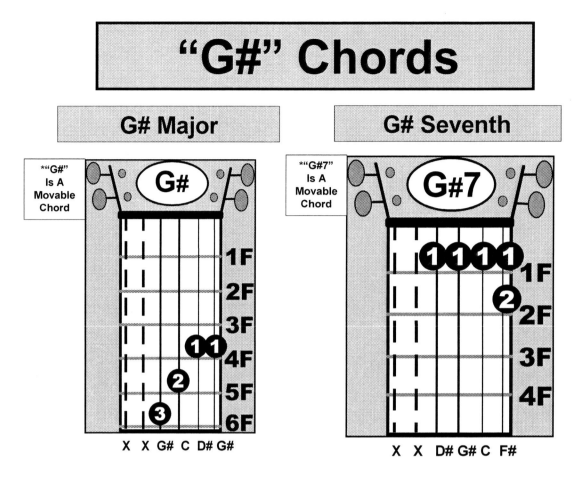

G#

1F
2F
3F
4F
5F
6F

X X G# C D# G#

G# Seventh

*"G#7" Is A Movable Chord

G#7

1F
2F
3F
4F

X X D# G# C F#

* G# CHORDS ARE ALSO CALLED A♭ CHORDS

G# Minor

*"G#m" Is A Movable Chord

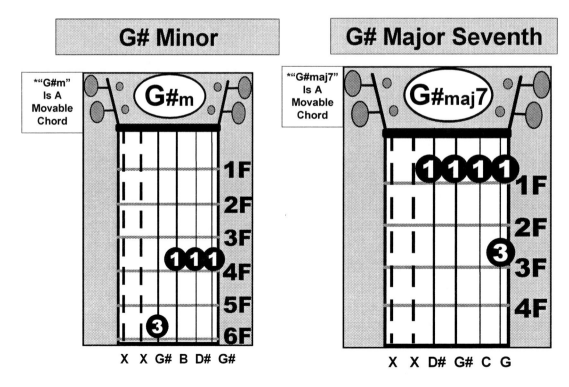

G#m

1F
2F
3F
4F
5F
6F

X X G# B D# G#

G# Major Seventh

*"G#maj7" Is A Movable Chord

G#maj7

1F
2F
3F
4F

X X D# G# C G

"B♭" Chords

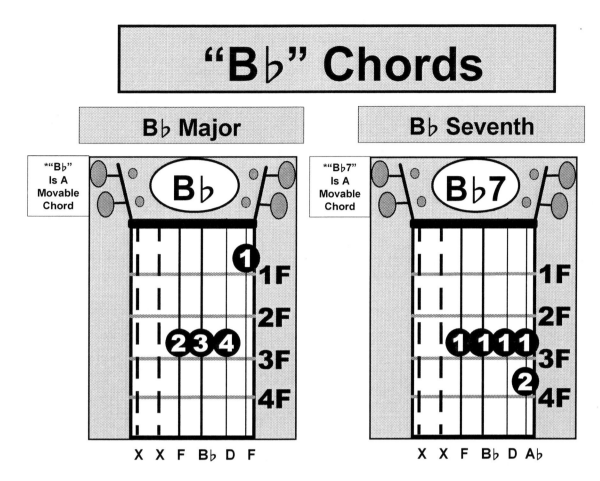

B♭ Major

*"B♭" Is A Movable Chord

B♭

1F
2F
3F
4F

X X F B♭ D F

B♭ Seventh

*"B♭7" Is A Movable Chord

B♭7

1F
2F
3F
4F

X X F B♭ D A♭

* **B♭** CHORDS ARE ALSO CALLED **A#** CHORDS

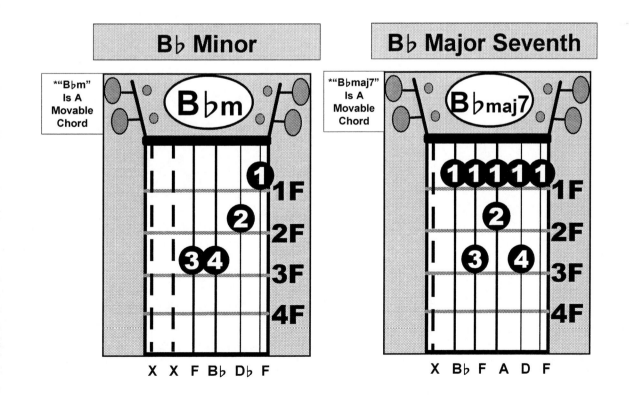

B♭ Minor

*"B♭m" Is A Movable Chord

B♭m

1F
2F
3F
4F

X X F B♭ D♭ F

B♭ Major Seventh

*"B♭maj7" Is A Movable Chord

B♭maj7

1F
2F
3F
4F

X B♭ F A D F

53

"C#" Chords

C# Major

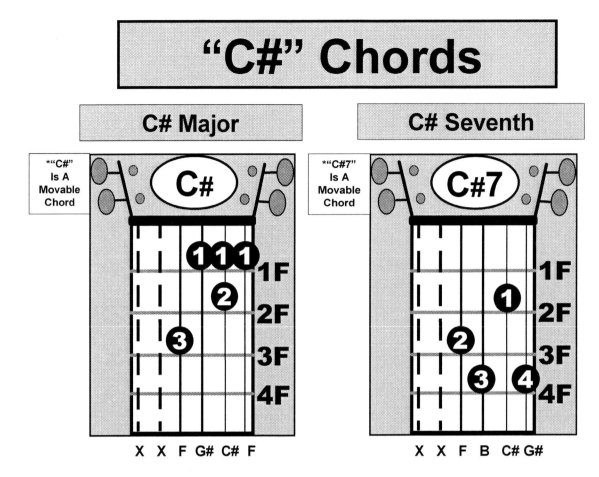

C#

1 1 1
2
3

1F
2F
3F
4F

X X F G# C# F

C# Seventh

C#7

1
2
3 4

1F
2F
3F
4F

X X F B C# G#

* C# CHORDS ARE ALSO CALLED D♭ CHORDS

C# Minor

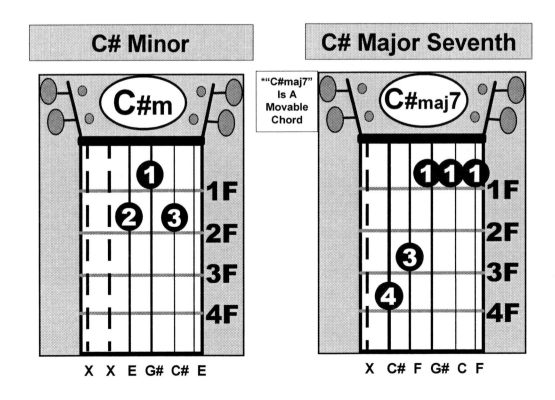

C#m

1
2 3

1F
2F
3F
4F

X X E G# C# E

C# Major Seventh

C#maj7

1 1 1
3
4

1F
2F
3F
4F

X C# F G# C F

"E♭" Chords

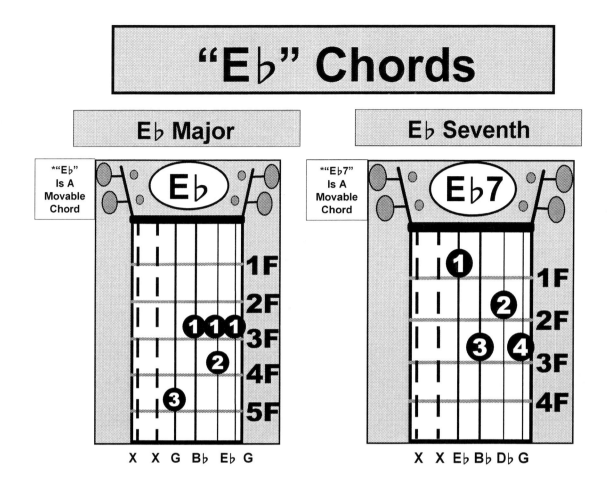

E♭ Major

*"E♭" Is A Movable Chord

E♭

1F
2F
3F   1 1 1
4F   2
5F   3

X X G B♭ E♭ G

E♭ Seventh

*"E♭7" Is A Movable Chord

E♭7

1F   1
2F   2
3F   3   4
4F

X X E♭ B♭ D♭ G

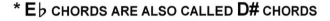

* E♭ CHORDS ARE ALSO CALLED D# CHORDS

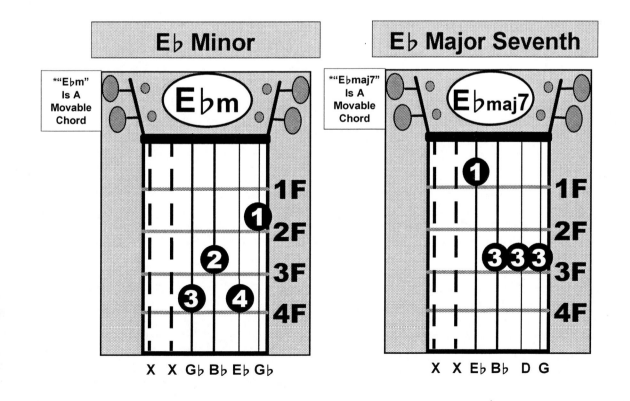

E♭ Minor

*"E♭m" Is A Movable Chord

E♭m

1F
2F   1
3F   2
4F   3   4

X X G♭ B♭ E♭ G♭

E♭ Major Seventh

*"E♭maj7" Is A Movable Chord

E♭maj7

1F   1
2F
3F   3 3 3
4F

X X E♭ B♭ D G

CHORD COMBINATION CHART

CREATING YOUR OWN CHORD COMBINATIONS IS EASY. BELOW IS A CHART MADE UP TWELVE INDIVIDUAL GROUPS OF CHORDS AND WITHIN EACH GROUP ARE THE CHORDS WHICH ARE COMMON TO EACH OTHER, IN OTHER WORDS, YOU CAN MIX ANY OF THE CHORDS WITHIN EACH GROUP TO CREATE VARIOUS CHORD COMBINATIONS, FOR EXAMPLE, FROM THE 1ST CHORD GROUP BELOW, PRACTICE PLAYING "C" TO "F" TO "G7" TO "G7," THEN REPEAT (SEE PAGE 19 TO VIEW CHORD DIAGRAM ILLUSTRATIONS OF THIS COMBINATION). THERE ARE NO SET ARRANGEMENTS THAT THE CHORDS MUST BE PLAYED IN OR NUMBER OF CHORDS THAT CAN BE USED, YOU CAN NOT GO WRONG, AS LONG AS THE CHORDS BEING PLAYED ARE IN THAT GROUP. THE SEVEN SHADED CHORD GROUPS ARE THE MOST COMMONLY PLAYED.

*ALL SEVENTH (7th) CHORDS ARE ALSO CALLED DOMINANT 7th CHORDS.

RELATED MAJOR, DOMINANT 7TH, & MINOR CHORD GROUPS							
CHORD GROUPS	Primary Major Chord (KEY)	Related Major Chord	Related Major Chord	Related Dominant 7th Chord	Related Minor Chord	Related Minor Chord	Related Dominant 7th Chord
1st Group	C	F	G	G7	Am	Dm	E7
2nd Group	A	D	E	E7	F#m	Bm	C#7
3rd Group	F	Bb	C	C7	Dm	Gm	A7
4th Group	G	C	D	D7	Em	Am	B7
5th Group	D	G	A	A7	Bm	Em	F#7
6th Group	E	A	B	B7	C#m	F#m	G#7
7th Group	B	E	F#	F#7	G#m	C#m	D#7
8th Group	F#	B	C#	C#7	D#m	G#m	A#7
9th Group	Ab	Db	Eb	Eb7	Fm	Bbm	C7
10th Group	Bb	Eb	F	F7	Gm	Cm	D7
11th Group	Db	Gb	Ab	Ab7	Bbm	Ebm	F7
12th Group	Eb	Ab	Bb	Bb7	Cm	Fm	G7

EXCUSE THE PUN, BUT DON'T FRET, IF YOU SHOULD COME ACROSS CHORDS SUCH AS "Am7" OR "Am6," SIMPLY SUBSTITUTE THESE CHORDS WITH A RELATED MINOR CHORD, IN THIS CASE, WITH THE "Am" CHORD (NOTE: ANY OTHER NOTATIONS AFTER THE FIRST LETTER OF A CHORD ARE CALLED "EXTENSIONS").

THE SAME CAN BE DONE WITH ANY OTHER CHORDS YOU MAY COME ACROSS, TAKE THE FIRST LETTER OF THE CHORD YOU ARE NOT FAMILIAR WITH AND SUBSTITUTE IT WITH THE FIRST LETTER OF A CHORD IN THIS BOOK THAT MOST CLOSELY RESEMBLES THE CHORD, FOR EXAMPLE, "A7+5" (Plus Sign Means Augmented) OR "A7-5" (Minus Sign Means Diminished), YOU WOULD PLAY THE "A7" CHORD. MORE EXAMPLES, "Em7" OR "Em6," SIMPLY SUBSTITUTE EITHER OF THESE CHORDS WITH AN "Em" CHORD.

SEVENTH (7TH) CHORDS

THE FOLLOWING PAGES ARE 7TH CHORDS IN A COMMONLY USED FINGER PATTERN.

THE 6TH STRING OPEN "E" NOTE IS A STRING YOU WILL NOT HAVE TO CONCERN YOURSELF WITH AS IT WILL ALWAYS BE MUTED BY THE TIP OF THE NUMBER 3 FINGER (RING FINGER) AND THE SAME GOES FOR THE 1ST STRING OPEN "E" NOTE AS IT WILL ALWAYS BE MUTED BY THE NUMBER 1 FINGER (INDEX FINGER), SO YOU WILL NOT HAVE TO SPEND TIME TRYING TO AVOID PLAYING THESE STRINGS. THE ONLY EXCEPTIONS TO THIS FINGER PATTERN ARE THE "B7" AND "C7" CHORDS. FOR THE "B7" CHORD, THE TIP OF THE NUMBER 2 (MIDDLE FINGER) WILL MUTE THE 6TH STRING OPEN "E" NOTE, ALSO PLACE THE NUMBER 4 (PINKY FINGER) ON THE 1ST STRING OPEN "E" NOTE, 2ND FRET. FOR THE "C7" CHORD, PLAY THE 1ST STRING OPEN "E" NOTE.

NOTICE THAT THE FINGER PATTERN OF THE SEVENTH CHORDS REMAIN THE SAME WHATEVER SEVENTH CHORD YOU ARE PLAYING, YOU ONLY HAVE TO SLIDE THIS FINGER PATTERN DOWN THE NECK TOWARD THE BODY OF THE GUITAR A FRET AT A TIME TO PRODUCE THE NEXT HIGHER SEVENTH CHORD.

* BE SURE TO CHECK OUT WHICH FRET THIS FINGER PATTERN SHOULD BE ON AS YOU PLAY THE SEVENTH CHORDS, THE FINGER PATTERN ALWAYS REMAINS THE SAME, HOWEVER, THE FRET LOCATION AND THE CHORD NAME OF THIS FINGER PATTERN WILL CHANGE FROM SEVENTH CHORD TO SEVENTH CHORD.

"7th" Chords

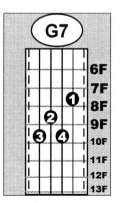

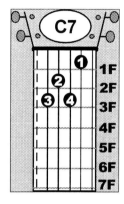

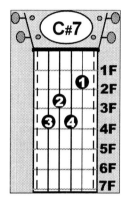

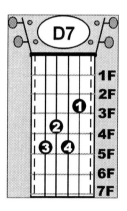

NOTE THAT THESE DIAGRAMS DEPICT THE UPPER AND LOWER HALF OF THE GUITAR NECK.
BE SURE FINGERS ARE PLACED ON THE PROPER FRET POSITIONS.

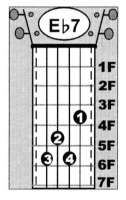

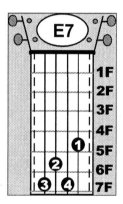

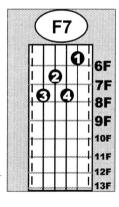

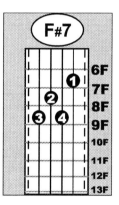

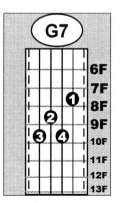

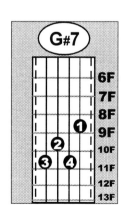

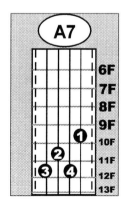

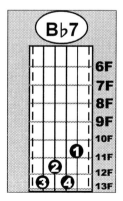

58

"7TH" CHORDS PRACTICE CHORD COMBINATION

BELOW IS A CHORD GROUP IN WHICH YOU CAN PRACTICE THE SEVENTH
CHORDS (7THS).

YOU CAN ALSO REPLACE THE SEVENTH CHORDS (7THS) WITH NINTH CHORDS
(9THS) OR MAJOR CHORDS. FOR EXAMPLE, THE 2ND AND 6TH CHORD IN THE
CHORD GROUP BELOW ARE "C7" CHORDS, THEY CAN BE REPLACED WITH "C9"
OR "C Major" CHORDS AND THE 5TH AND 8TH CHORD WHICH ARE "D7" CHORDS
CAN BE REPLACED WITH "D9" OR "D Major" CHORDS.

SLOWLY OR MODERATELY STRUM <u>EACH</u> CHORD YOU PLAY AT LEAST FOUR
TIMES, TO A COUNT OF FOUR, TRY TAPPING YOUR FOOT TO KEEP COUNT
(1 ANNA 2 ANNA 3 ANNA 4), OR UNTIL YOU FIND WHAT IS COMFORTABLE FOR
YOU. (THE "NUMBER" COUNT IS WHEN YOUR FOOT TAPS THE FLOOR, THE
"ANNA" COUNT IS WHEN YOUR FOOT IS RAISED).

PRACTICE CHORD COMBINATION

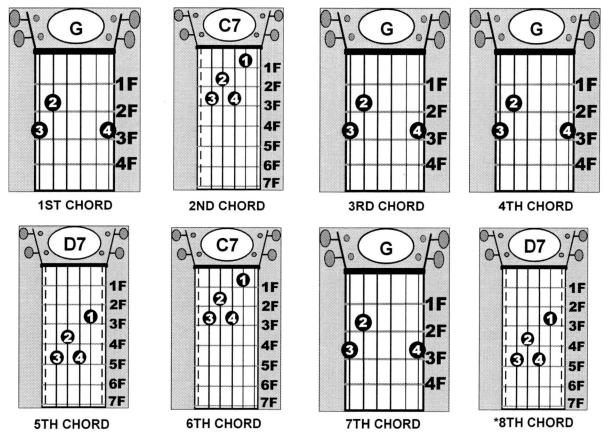

AFTER PLAYING THE *8TH CHORD IN THIS GROUP,
SIMPLY REPEAT THIS ENTIRE CHORD GROUP.....

MORE ABOUT "7TH" CHORDS

SEVENTH CHORDS (7THS) ARE OFTEN PLAYED IN A THREE CHORD PROGRESSION (The movement from one chord to another is called a chord progression). BELOW IS A LIST OF COMMONLY PLAYED CHORD PROGRESSIONS IN A GROUP OF EIGHT CHORDS, USING A MAJOR CHORD ALONG WITH TWO OF THE RELATIVE 7TH CHORDS. VISUALLY MAP THESE PROGRESSIONS OUT ON THE "GUITAR STRING NOTE NAMES" DIAGRAM ON PAGE 10 (MAP THE CHORD PROGRESSION BY USING THE FIRST LETTER OF EACH CHORD) AND YOU WILL NOTICE A PATTERN. THE 2nd Chord Group BELOW IS ILLUSTRATED ON PAGE 59.

SLOWLY OR MODERATELY STRUM <u>EACH</u> CHORD YOU PLAY AT LEAST FOUR TIMES, TO A COUNT OF FOUR, TRY TAPPING YOUR FOOT TO KEEP COUNT (1 ANNA 2 ANNA 3 ANNA 4), OR UNTIL YOU FIND WHAT IS COMFORTABLE FOR YOU. (THE "NUMBER" COUNT IS WHEN YOUR FOOT TAPS THE FLOOR, THE "ANNA" COUNT IS WHEN YOUR FOOT IS RAISED).

7TH CHORD PROGRESSIONS

Chord Group	1st Chord	2nd Chord	3rd & 4th Chord	5th Chord	6th Chord	7th Chord	8th Chord	
1st Chord Group	F# Major	B7	F# Major	C#7	B7	F# Major	C#7	Then Repeat
2nd Chord Group	G Major	C7	G Major	D7	C7	G Major	D7	Then Repeat
3rd Chord Group	G# Major	C#7	G# Major	Eb7	C#7	G# Major	Eb7	Then Repeat
4th Chord Group	A Major	D7	A Major	E7	D7	A Major	E7	Then Repeat
5th Chord Group	Bb Major	Eb7	Bb Major	F7	Eb7	Bb Major	F7	Then Repeat
6th Chord Group	B Major	E7	B Major	F#7	E7	B Major	F#7	Then Repeat
7th Chord Group	C Major	F7	C Major	G7	F7	C Major	G7	Then Repeat
8th Chord Group	C# Major	F#7	C# Major	G#7	F#7	C# Major	G#7	Then Repeat
9th Chord Group	D Major	G7	D Major	A7	G7	D Major	A7	Then Repeat
10th Chord Group	Eb Major	G#7	Eb Major	Bb7	G#7	Eb Major	Bb7	Then Repeat
11th Chord Group	E Major	A7	E Major	B7	A7	E Major	B7	Then Repeat
12th Chord Group	F Major	Bb7	F Major	C7	Bb7	F Major	C7	Then Repeat

NINTH (9TH) CHORDS

THE FOLLOWING PAGES ARE 9TH CHORDS IN A COMMONLY USED FINGER PATTERN.

THE 6TH STRING OPEN "E" NOTE IS A STRING YOU WILL NOT HAVE TO CONCERN YOURSELF WITH AS IT WILL ALWAYS BE MUTED BY ALLOWING THE TIP OF THE NUMBER 2 FINGER (MIDDLE FINGER) TO LIGHTLY TOUCH THE 6TH STRING, SO YOU WILL NOT HAVE TO SPEND TIME TRYING TO AVOID PLAYING THIS STRING.

NOTICE THAT THE FINGER PATTERN OF THE NINTH CHORDS REMAIN THE SAME WHATEVER NINTH CHORD YOU ARE PLAYING, YOU ONLY HAVE TO SLIDE THIS FINGER PATTERN DOWN THE NECK TOWARD THE BODY OF THE GUITAR A FRET AT A TIME TO PRODUCE THE NEXT HIGHER NINTH CHORD.

* BE SURE TO CHECK OUT WHICH FRET THIS FINGER PATTERN SHOULD BE ON AS YOU PLAY THE NINTH CHORDS, THE FINGER PATTERN ALWAYS REMAINS THE SAME, HOWEVER, THE FRET LOCATION AND THE CHORD NAME OF THIS FINGER PATTERN WILL CHANGE FROM NINTH CHORD TO NINTH CHORD.

"9th" Chords

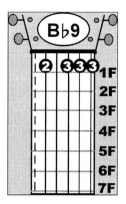
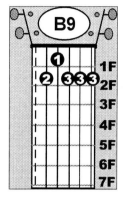
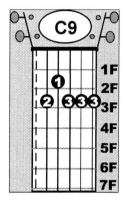
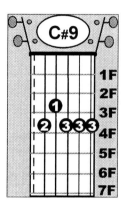

NOTE THAT THESE DIAGRAMS DEPICT THE UPPER AND LOWER HALF OF THE GUITAR NECK.
BE SURE FINGERS ARE PLACED ON THE PROPER FRET POSITIONS.

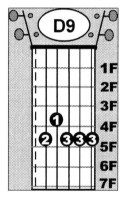
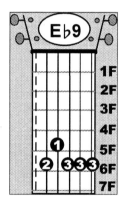
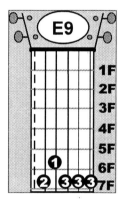
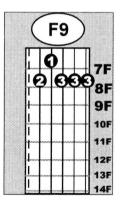

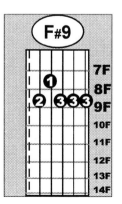
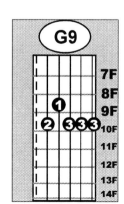
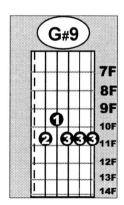
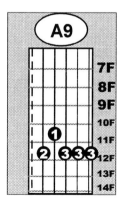

"9TH" CHORDS PRACTICE CHORD COMBINATION

BELOW IS A CHORD GROUP IN WHICH YOU CAN PRACTICE THE NINTH CHORDS (9THS).

YOU CAN ALSO REPLACE THE NINTH CHORDS (9THS) WITH SEVENTH (7THS) OR MAJOR CHORDS. FOR EXAMPLE, THE 2ND AND 6TH CHORD IN THE CHORD GROUP BELOW ARE "C9" CHORDS, THEY CAN BE REPLACED WITH "C7" OR "C Major" CHORDS AND THE 5TH AND 8TH CHORD WHICH ARE "D9" CHORDS CAN BE REPLACED WITH "D7" OR "D Major" CHORDS.

SLOWLY OR MODERATELY STRUM <u>EACH</u> CHORD YOU PLAY AT LEAST FOUR TIMES, TO A COUNT OF FOUR, TRY TAPPING YOUR FOOT TO KEEP COUNT (1 ANNA 2 ANNA 3 ANNA 4), OR UNTIL YOU FIND WHAT IS COMFORTABLE FOR YOU. (THE "NUMBER" COUNT IS WHEN YOUR FOOT TAPS THE FLOOR, THE "ANNA" COUNT IS WHEN YOUR FOOT IS RAISED).

PRACTICE CHORD COMBINATION

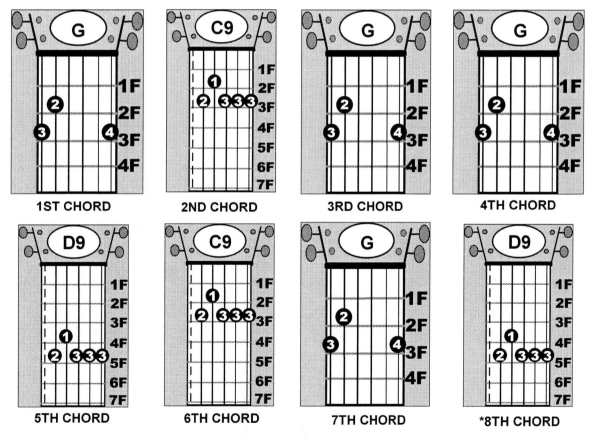

AFTER PLAYING THE *8TH CHORD IN THIS GROUP,
SIMPLY REPEAT THIS ENTIRE CHORD GROUP.....

MORE ABOUT "9TH" CHORDS

NINTH CHORDS (9THS) ARE OFTEN PLAYED IN A THREE CHORD PROGRESSION (The movement from one chord to another is called a chord progression). BELOW IS A LIST OF COMMONLY PLAYED CHORD PROGRESSIONS IN A GROUP OF EIGHT CHORDS, USING A MAJOR CHORD ALONG WITH TWO OF THE RELATIVE 9TH CHORDS. VISUALLY MAP THESE PROGRESSIONS OUT ON THE "GUITAR STRING NOTE NAMES" DIAGRAM ON PAGE 10 (MAP THE CHORD PROGRESSION BY USING THE FIRST LETTER OF EACH CHORD) AND YOU WILL NOTICE A PATTERN. THE 3rd Chord Group BELOW IS ILLUSTRATED ON THE PAGE 63.

SLOWLY OR MODERATELY STRUM EACH CHORD YOU PLAY AT LEAST FOUR TIMES, TO A COUNT OF FOUR, TRY TAPPING YOUR FOOT TO KEEP COUNT (1 ANNA 2 ANNA 3 ANNA 4), OR UNTIL YOU FIND WHAT IS COMFORTABLE FOR YOU. (THE "NUMBER" COUNT IS WHEN YOUR FOOT TAPS THE FLOOR, THE "ANNA" COUNT IS WHEN YOUR FOOT IS RAISED).

9TH CHORD PROGRESSIONS

Chord Group	1st Chord	2nd Chord	3rd & 4th Chord	5th Chord	6th Chord	7th Chord	8th Chord	
1st Chord Group	F Major	B♭9	F Major	C9	B♭9	F Major	C7 or C9	Then Repeat
2nd Chord Group	F# Major	B9	F# Major	C#9	B9	F# Major	C#7 or C#9	Then Repeat
3rd Chord Group	G Major	C9	G Major	D9	C9	G Major	D7 or D9	Then Repeat
4th Chord Group	G# Major	C#9	G# Major	E♭9	C#9	G# Major	E♭7 or E♭9	Then Repeat
5th Chord Group	A Major	D9	A Major	E9	D9	A Major	E7 or E9	Then Repeat
6th Chord Group	B♭ Major	E♭9	B♭ Major	F9	E♭9	B♭ Major	F7 or F9	Then Repeat
7th Chord Group	B Major	E9	B Major	F#9	E9	B Major	F#7 or F#9	Then Repeat
8th Chord Group	C Major	F9	C Major	G9	F9	C Major	G7 or G9	Then Repeat
9th Chord Group	C# Major	F#9	C# Major	G#9	F#9	C# Major	G#7 or G#9	Then Repeat
10th Chord Group	D Major	G9	D Major	A9	G9	D Major	A7 or A9	Then Repeat
11th Chord Group	E♭Major	G#9	E♭ Major	B♭9	G#9	E♭ Major	B♭7 or B♭9	Then Repeat
12th Chord Group	E Major	A9	E Major	B9	A9	E Major	B7 or B9	Then Repeat

HOW TO READ & USE TABLATURE

HOW TO READ & USE TABLATURE

If reading music is not your "cup of tea," you can utilize **Tablature.** Although tablature carries a strong resemblance to standard musical notation, that is where the similarities end. Each horizontal line of the **"Tab"** (Tablature) represents a string on the guitar - **NOT DEGREES OF PITCH** (i.e., notes on a staff) as presented in standard notation. That is why tablature has six (6) horizontal lines (strings 1 through 6), while standard notation on the staff uses five (5) lines. The top line on the tablature represents the first string on the guitar and proceeds in sequence to the sixth string on the bottom of the tablature.

Tablature also differs from standard notation in that tablature incorporates the use of **NUMBERS,** rather than notes to identify a specific note or notes to be played on the guitar. Thus, (using the Tab on Page 67) a number **"5"** placed on the bottom line (6th string) of the **Tab** means; **press down on the (5th) fret of the sixth (6th) string on the guitar fingerboard and play (pluck) the sixth (6th) string.** Similarly, a **"7"** placed on the bottom line (6th string) of the **Tab** means; **press down on the (7th) fret of the sixth (6th) string then play (pluck) the sixth (6th) string on the guitar. Note:** Whenever you see an **"O"** placed on anyone of the strings, this simply means to play (pluck) that particular string "Open" on the guitar **(no fingering on the frets).**

To indicate which fingers to use, we placed a small oval shape **"Finger Identifier,"** with the correct finger(s), next to the **BOLD** fret number. The **GRAY** colored oval shape numbers indicate the root notes. Directly above the **Tablature** you will find the same corresponding note(s) written in standard musical notation.

On Page 67, are examples of the way the same "A" Major Scale looks in "Standard Notation," **"Tablature"** and on the "Guitar Neck Finger Board." Also, there is an example of how a chord can be translated to Tablature. There are more practice tablatures and more about scale patterns available in:

The "Next Stage" Guitar Book -
Learn How To Play Scale Patterns & Tabs Easily & Quickly!

HOW TO READ & USE TABLATURE

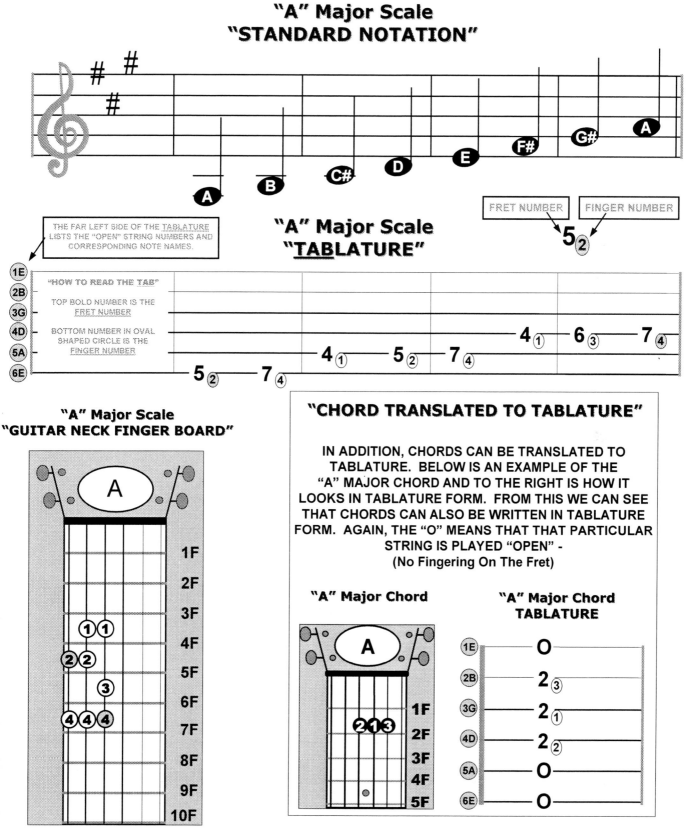

PRACTICE SCALE PATTERNS
(Major & Minor Pentatonics & "Blues Scale")
With Chord Progressions

The following pages will introduce you to some basic practice scale patterns with chord progressions so that you can get a feel of playing lead guitar. The scale patterns are presented in double octaves which will allow for more notes to be played in various pitches. Below will explain how these scale patterns are to be played.

1.   "SCALE PATH" DIAGRAM:

This method is best described as the **"One Picture Paints A Thousand Words"** method. Each scale is symbolically drawn on an illustrated picture of a guitar neck. A small circle(s) depicted on the fret(s) tells us where on the fingerboard we play the notes of the scale. We will call this small circle(s) the **"Finger/Note Identifier"** because it tells us the correct finger to use and the name of the note.

The fret numbers are indicated along the right side of the scale path diagram (i.e., 1F, 2F, 3F....etc.). You should begin playing the scales (see **"Scale Path"**) starting with the "root" note. The root note will be the lowest pitched note on the **LEFT** side of the **"Scale Path"** diagram. The root note(s) will also be "colored" **GRAY** so you can easily identify them from the other notes in the scale. From that gray colored root note, proceed in (alphabetical) order through each successively higher note on each string until you reach the final or highest pitch root note in the scale (it too will be "colored" **GRAY**) on the **RIGHT** side of the **"Scale Path"** diagram. To descend, just reverse the process.

Another way to view this process is to think that the scales always (for now) start on the heavier gauge strings and move toward the lighter or thinner gauge strings, then reverse and proceed back to the beginning.

2. STANDARD MUSICAL NOTATION:

If you can read "standard musical notation," you may find that is an ideal place to start. Again, all scales begin in the ascending mode; that is, the first note (the root note) of the scale will be the lowest note in terms of pitch and proceed in sequence (alphabetically) until the highest note of the scale is reached. The notes on the staff are in relationship to the **"Finger/Note Identifiers"** (numbers & notes) on the **"Scale Path"** and the oval **"Finger Identifiers"** depicted in the **Tablature** directly below the Staff.

MOVABLE SCALE PATTERNS:

The beautiful feature of the scales, as presented in this book, is that they are **ALL "Movable Scales."** That is to say you can change to a different scale other than the one illustrated on the page (i.e., "A" Major Scale to a "G" Major Scale). This can be accomplished by simply starting any of the **"Scale Patterns"** on a different fret or root note other than the one depicted in the book. Nothing changes other than the frets (and the notes) that the original scale was played on. Just remember to keep your fingering the same as in the original **"Scale Pattern."** By learning to start the scales on different frets, allows you to play these scales in different Keys.

"TWELVE BAR CHORD PROGRESSIONS"
TO PLAY ALONG WITH SCALES:

You will find a standard **"Twelve Bar Chord Progression"** that can be used as an accompaniment for the **Major Pentatonic, Minor Pentatonic** and **"Blues Scale."** The chord progression is written in the Key of "A," but you can play it in a different Key once you learn to "move" the scale and transpose the chords to another key. Once you achieve proficiency executing these scales, try recording yourself on tape so you can play the twelve bar chord progression along with the scales. Conversely, try recording the twelve bar chord progression and play the scales "over the chords." Even better, get a friend to play the chords while you execute the scales. Most of all, have fun.

"A" Major Pentatonic Scale
(Double Octave)

"SCALE PATH"

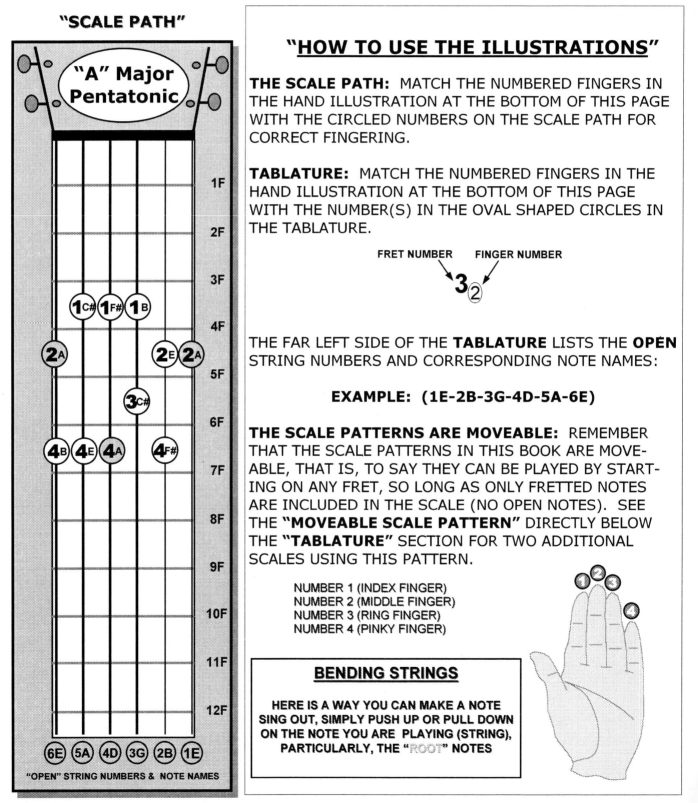

"HOW TO USE THE ILLUSTRATIONS"

THE SCALE PATH: MATCH THE NUMBERED FINGERS IN THE HAND ILLUSTRATION AT THE BOTTOM OF THIS PAGE WITH THE CIRCLED NUMBERS ON THE SCALE PATH FOR CORRECT FINGERING.

TABLATURE: MATCH THE NUMBERED FINGERS IN THE HAND ILLUSTRATION AT THE BOTTOM OF THIS PAGE WITH THE NUMBER(S) IN THE OVAL SHAPED CIRCLES IN THE TABLATURE.

FRET NUMBER   FINGER NUMBER

3②

THE FAR LEFT SIDE OF THE **TABLATURE** LISTS THE **OPEN** STRING NUMBERS AND CORRESPONDING NOTE NAMES:

EXAMPLE: (1E-2B-3G-4D-5A-6E)

THE SCALE PATTERNS ARE MOVEABLE: REMEMBER THAT THE SCALE PATTERNS IN THIS BOOK ARE MOVEABLE, THAT IS, TO SAY THEY CAN BE PLAYED BY STARTING ON ANY FRET, SO LONG AS ONLY FRETTED NOTES ARE INCLUDED IN THE SCALE (NO OPEN NOTES). SEE THE **"MOVEABLE SCALE PATTERN"** DIRECTLY BELOW THE **"TABLATURE"** SECTION FOR TWO ADDITIONAL SCALES USING THIS PATTERN.

NUMBER 1 (INDEX FINGER)
NUMBER 2 (MIDDLE FINGER)
NUMBER 3 (RING FINGER)
NUMBER 4 (PINKY FINGER)

BENDING STRINGS

HERE IS A WAY YOU CAN MAKE A NOTE SING OUT, SIMPLY PUSH UP OR PULL DOWN ON THE NOTE YOU ARE PLAYING (STRING), PARTICULARLY, THE "ROOT" NOTES

"A" Major Pentatonic Scale
(Double Octave)
Standard Notation & Tablature

"STANDARD NOTATION"

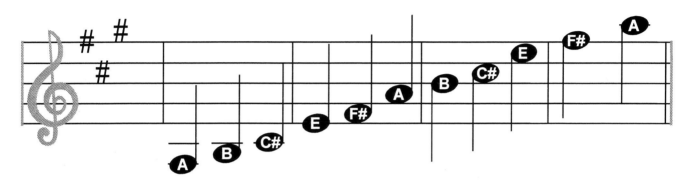

"TABLATURE"

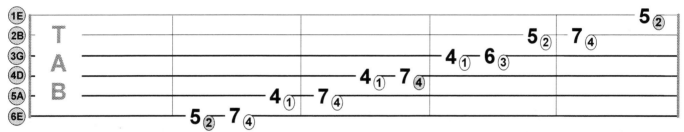

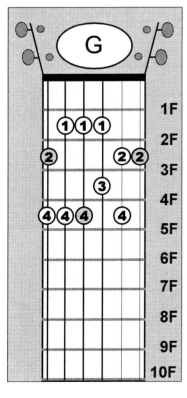

"MOVEABLE SCALE PATTERNS"

THE DIAGRAMS TO THE LEFT AND RIGHT SHOW HOW THE SAME **"SCALE PATTERN"** CAN BE MOVED ALONG THE GUITAR NECK SO THAT THE SCALE CAN BE PLAYED IN A NEW POSITION AND KEY.

LEFT - THE **"SCALE PATTERN"** HAS BEEN MOVED DOWN THE NECK TWO (2) FRETS (LOWER IN PITCH).

RIGHT - THE **"SCALE PATTERN"** HAS BEEN MOVED UP THE NECK THREE (3) FRETS (HIGHER IN PITCH).

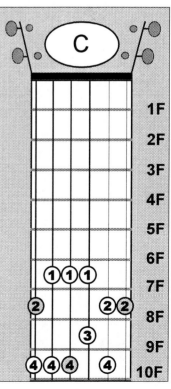

"A" Major Pentatonic Scale
(Double Octave)

"SCALE PATH"

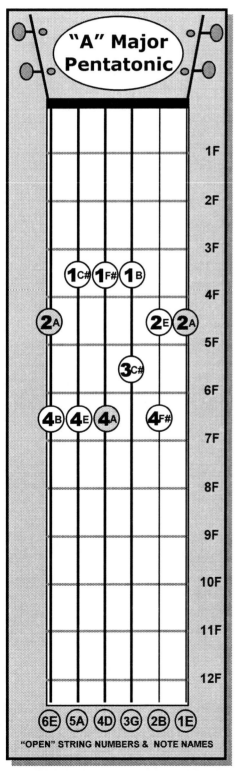

MAJOR PENTATONIC SCALE
&
TWELVE BAR CHORD PROGRESSION

IF YOU DESIRE TO MOVE THE "A" MAJOR PENTATONIC SCALE PATTERN TO ANOTHER POSITION ON THE GUITAR NECK, LET'S SAY THREE (3) FRETS UP THE GUITAR NECK (HIGHER IN PITCH), THE SCALE WOULD THEN BECOME A "C" MAJOR PENTATONIC SCALE. REMEMBER WHEN YOU CHANGE THE KEY OF THE SCALE, YOU MUST CHANGE THE CORRESPONDING CHORDS. IN THIS CASE, THE NEW CHORD PROGRESSION CAN BE:

C, F, C, C7, F, Fm, C, A7, D7, G7, C, G7

REMEMBER, ONCE YOU MEMORIZE AND MASTER THE PENTATONIC PATTERNS CONTAINED IN THIS BOOK, YOU CAN USE THE NOTES IN THE **PENTATONIC SCALE** TO COMPOSE SIMPLE SONGS AND MELODIES BY VARYING THE ORDER OF NOTES PLAYED IN THE SCALE.

ON THE NEXT PAGE, THE LAST CHORD IN THE PROGRESSION IS CALLED THE "TURNAROUND" CHORD. IT WILL LEAD YOU BACK TO THE BEGINNING OF THE CHORD PROGRESSION IF YOU WANT TO CONTINUE PLAYING THE PROGRESSION. WHEN YOU ARE READY TO END THE PROGRESSION, CHANGE THE "E7" TURNAROUND CHORD TO AN "A" CHORD AND END THE PROGRESSION ON THE FOURTH (4TH) COUNT.

"A" Major Pentatonic Scale (Double Octave)
Twelve Bar Practice Chord Progression

The Staffs below are divided into four bars (measures) by vertical lines (called "Bar Lines"), and within each bar is a chord. Strum each chord you play at least four times, to a count of four. Try tapping your foot to keep count (1 anna 2 anna 3 anna 4). The "number" count is when your foot taps the floor, the "anna" count is when your foot is raised. You may wish to record this chord progression or have someone else play it while you practice the scale along with the chords. Some of the chords repeat. When this occurs, simply play that chord for four more counts. Repeat the progression after the 12th Chord, (Turnaround Chord).

DO NOT PLAY BROKEN LINE STRINGS, HOWEVER PLAY ALL OTHER STRINGS IN CHORDS

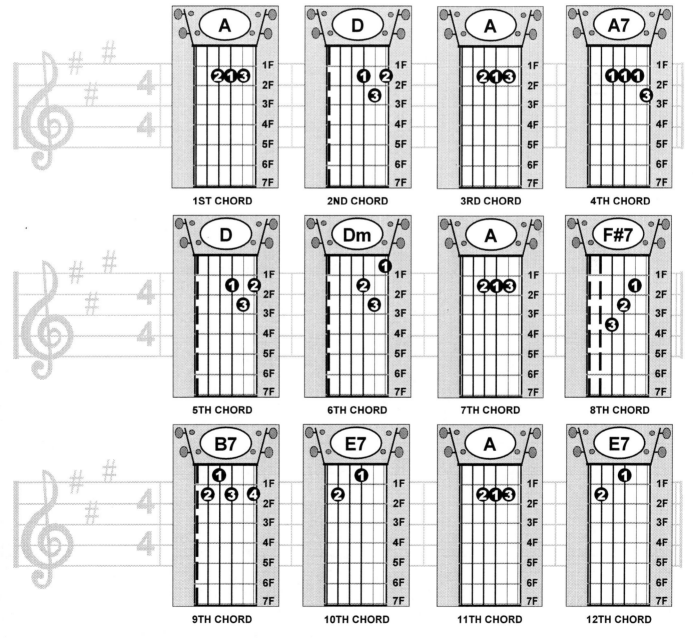

"A" Minor Pentatonic Scale
(Double Octave)

"SCALE PATH"

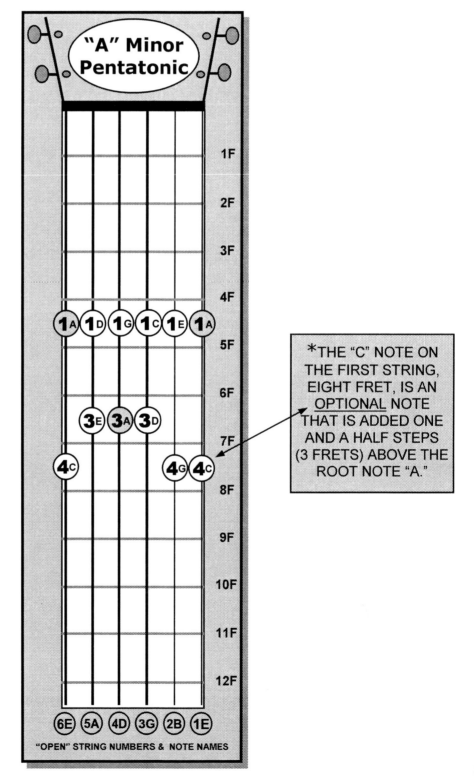

*THE "C" NOTE ON THE FIRST STRING, EIGHT FRET, IS AN OPTIONAL NOTE THAT IS ADDED ONE AND A HALF STEPS (3 FRETS) ABOVE THE ROOT NOTE "A."

"A" Minor Pentatonic Scale
(Double Octave)
Standard Notation & Tablature

"STANDARD NOTATION"

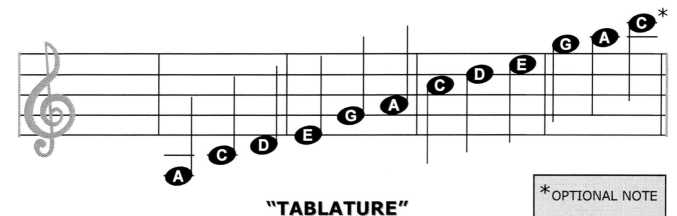

*OPTIONAL NOTE

"TABLATURE"

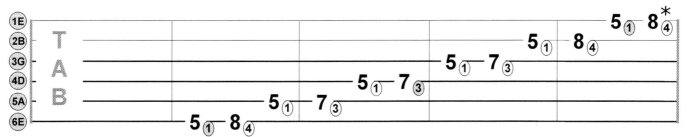

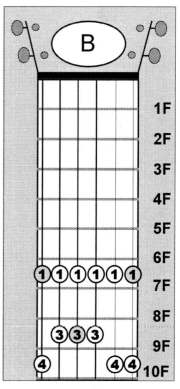

"MOVEABLE SCALE PATTERN"

THE DIAGRAMS TO THE LEFT AND RIGHT SHOW HOW THE SAME **"SCALE PATTERN"** CAN BE MOVED ALONG THE GUITAR NECK SO THAT THE SCALE CAN BE PLAYED IN A NEW POSITION AND KEY.

LEFT - THE **"SCALE PATTERN"** HAS BEEN MOVED DOWN THE NECK TWO (2) FRETS (LOWER IN PITCH).

RIGHT - THE **"SCALE PATTERN"** HAS BEEN MOVED UP THE NECK TWO (2) FRETS (HIGHER IN PITCH).

"A" Minor Pentatonic Scale
(Double Octave)

"SCALE PATH"

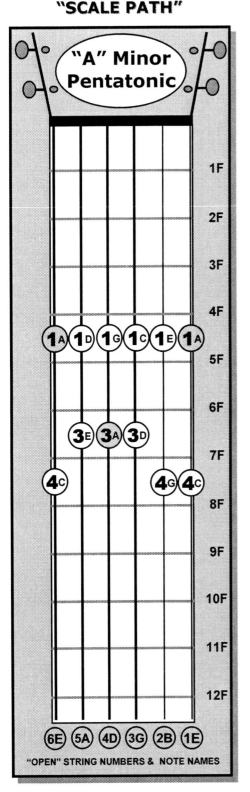

MINOR PENTATONIC SCALE
&
TWELVE BAR CHORD PROGRESSION

IF YOU DESIRE TO MOVE THE "A" MINOR PENTATONIC SCALE PATTERN TO ANOTHER POSITION ON THE GUITAR NECK, LET'S SAY THREE (3) FRETS UP THE GUITAR NECK (HIGHER IN PITCH), THE SCALE WOULD THEN BECOME A "C" MINOR PENTATONIC SCALE. REMEMBER WHEN YOU CHANGE THE KEY OF THE SCALE, YOU MUST CHANGE THE CORRESPONDING CHORDS. IN THIS CASE, THE NEW CHORD PROGRESSION CAN BE:

C, F, C, C7, F, F7, C, C7, G7, F, C, G7

REMEMBER, ONCE YOU MEMORIZE AND MASTER THE PENTATONIC PATTERNS CONTAINED IN THIS BOOK, YOU CAN USE THE NOTES IN THE **PENTATONIC SCALE** TO COMPOSE SIMPLE SONGS AND MELODIES BY VARYING THE ORDER OF NOTES PLAYED IN THE SCALE.

ON THE NEXT PAGE, THE LAST CHORD IN THE PROGRESSION IS CALLED THE "TURNAROUND" CHORD. IT WILL LEAD YOU BACK TO THE BEGINNING OF THE CHORD PROGRESSION IF YOU WANT TO CONTINUE PLAYING THE PROGRESSION. WHEN YOU ARE READY TO END THE PROGRESSION, CHANGE THE "E7" TURNAROUND CHORD TO AN "A" CHORD AND END THE PROGRESSION ON THE FOURTH (4TH) COUNT.

"A" Minor Pentatonic Scale (Double Octave)
Twelve Bar Practice Chord Progression

The Staffs below are divided into four bars (measures) by vertical lines (called "Bar Lines"), and within each bar is a chord. Strum each chord you play at least four times, to a count of four. Try tapping your foot to keep count (1 anna 2 anna 3 anna 4). The "number" count is when your foot taps the floor, the "anna" count is when your foot is raised. You may wish to record this chord progression or have someone else play it while you practice the scale along with the chords. Some of the chords repeat. When this occurs, simply play that chord for four more counts. Repeat the progression after the 12th Chord, (Turnaround Chord).

DO NOT PLAY BROKEN LINE STRINGS, HOWEVER PLAY ALL OTHER STRINGS IN CHORDS

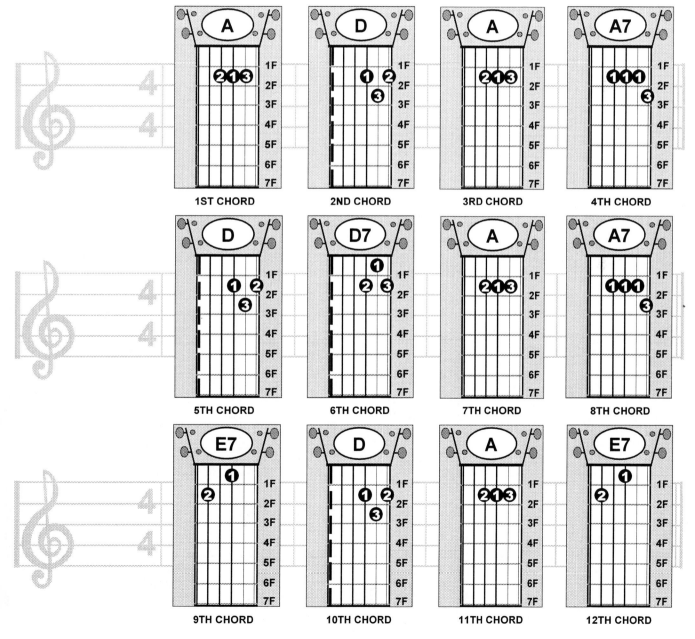

"Blues Scale" In "A"
(Double Octave)
(Based on the Minor Pentatonic Scale)

"SCALE PATH"

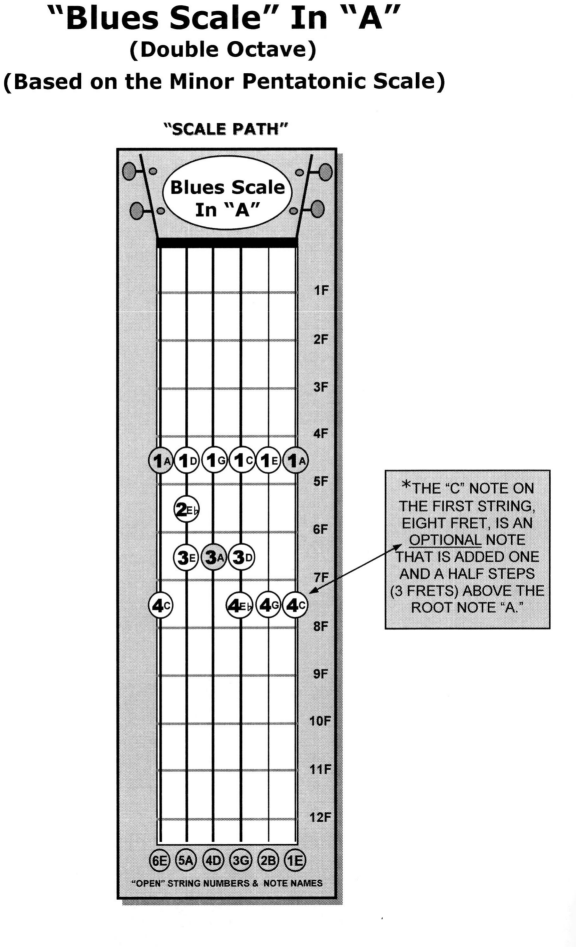

*THE "C" NOTE ON THE FIRST STRING, EIGHT FRET, IS AN OPTIONAL NOTE THAT IS ADDED ONE AND A HALF STEPS (3 FRETS) ABOVE THE ROOT NOTE "A."

"Blues Scale" In "A"
(Double Octave)
Standard Notation & Tablature

"STANDARD NOTATION"

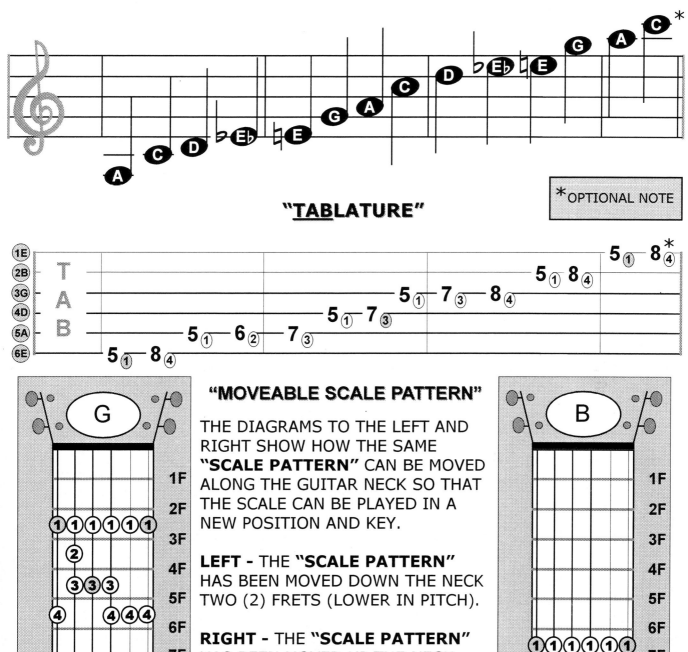

*OPTIONAL NOTE

"TABLATURE"

"MOVEABLE SCALE PATTERN"

THE DIAGRAMS TO THE LEFT AND RIGHT SHOW HOW THE SAME **"SCALE PATTERN"** CAN BE MOVED ALONG THE GUITAR NECK SO THAT THE SCALE CAN BE PLAYED IN A NEW POSITION AND KEY.

LEFT - THE **"SCALE PATTERN"** HAS BEEN MOVED DOWN THE NECK TWO (2) FRETS (LOWER IN PITCH).

RIGHT - THE **"SCALE PATTERN"** HAS BEEN MOVED UP THE NECK TWO (2) FRETS (HIGHER IN PITCH).

"Blues Scale" In "A"
(Double Octave)
(Based on the Minor Pentatonic Scale)

"SCALE PATH"

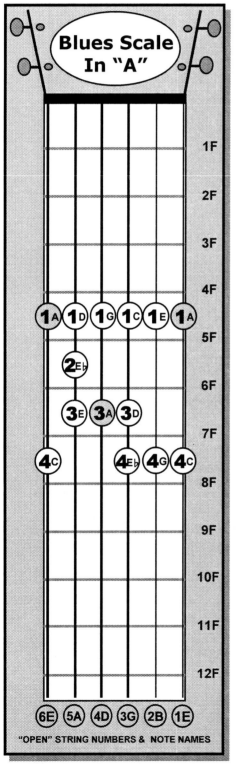

Blues Scale In "A"

1F
2F
3F
4F

1A 1D 1G 1C 1E 1A

5F

2E♭

6F

3E 3A 3D

7F

4C 4E♭ 4G 4C

8F
9F
10F
11F
12F

6E 5A 4D 3G 2B 1E

"OPEN" STRING NUMBERS & NOTE NAMES

"BLUES SCALE" IN "A"
&
TWELVE BAR CHORD PROGRESSION

IF YOU DESIRE TO MOVE THE "BLUES SCALE" IN THE "A" PATTERN TO ANOTHER POSITION ON THE GUITAR NECK, LET'S SAY THREE (3) FRETS UP THE GUITAR NECK (HIGHER IN PITCH), THE SCALE WOULD THEN BECOME A "BLUES SCALE" IN "C". REMEMBER WHEN YOU CHANGE THE KEY OF THE SCALE, YOU MUST CHANGE THE CORRESPONDING CHORDS. IN THIS CASE, THE NEW CHORD PROGRESSION CAN BE:

C, C, C, C7, F, F, C, C7, G7, F, C, G7

REMEMBER, ONCE YOU MEMORIZE AND MASTER THE PENTATONIC PATTERNS CONTAINED IN THIS BOOK, YOU CAN USE THE NOTES IN THE **PENTATONIC SCALE** TO COMPOSE SIMPLE SONGS AND MELODIES BY VARYING THE ORDER OF NOTES PLAYED IN THE SCALE.

ON THE NEXT PAGE, THE LAST CHORD IN THE PROGRESSION IS CALLED THE "TURNAROUND" CHORD. IT WILL LEAD YOU BACK TO THE BEGINNING OF THE CHORD PROGRESSION IF YOU WANT TO CONTINUE PLAYING THE PROGRESSION. WHEN YOU ARE READY TO END THE PROGRESSION, CHANGE THE "E7" TURNAROUND CHORD TO AN "A" CHORD AND END THE PROGRESSION ON THE FOURTH (4TH) COUNT.

"Blues Scale" In "A" (Double Octave)
Twelve Bar Practice Chord Progression

The Staffs below are divided into four bars (measures) by vertical lines (called "Bar Lines"), and within each bar is a chord. Strum each chord you play at least four times, to a count of four. Try tapping your foot to keep count (1 anna 2 anna 3 anna 4). The "number" count is when your foot taps the floor, the "anna" count is when your foot is raised. You may wish to record this chord progression or have someone else play it while you practice the scale along with the chords. Some of the chords repeat. When this occurs, simply play that chord for four more counts. Repeat the progression after the 12th Chord, (Turnaround Chord).

__YOU CAN SUBSTITUTE THE "D9th" CHORD FOR THE "D" CHORD & THE "E9th" FOR THE "E7th"__
__DO__ __NOT__ __PLAY__ __BROKEN__ __LINE__ __STRINGS__, HOWEVER PLAY ALL OTHER STRINGS IN CHORDS

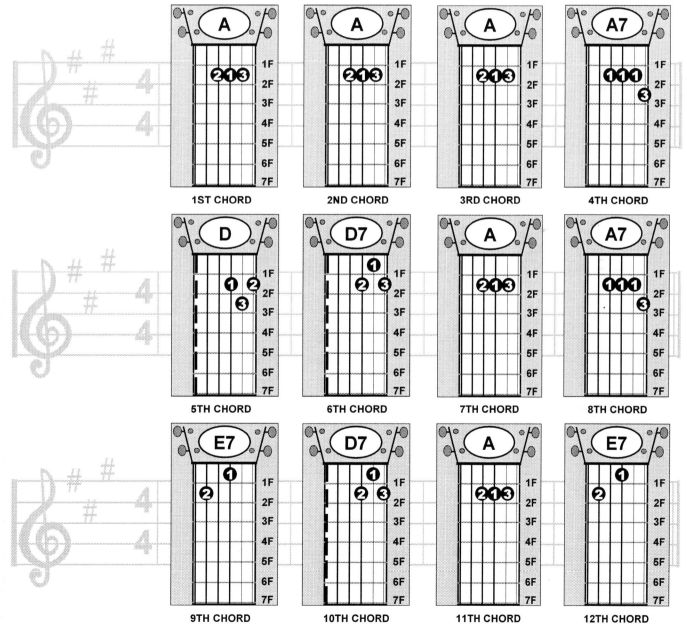

MORE "HOW TO PLAY GUITAR" BOOKS

ON ANOTHER NOTE, IF YOU WOULD LIKE TO LEARN HOW TO PLAY SCALE PATTERNS & TABS
BE SURE TO GET A COPY OF:

THE "NEXT STAGE" GUITAR BOOK -
LEARN HOW TO PLAY SCALE PATTERNS & TABS EASILY & QUICKLY!

ALSO AVAILABLE IS THE QUICK CHORD REFERENCE CHART:

THE "FIRST STAGE" GUITAR CHORD CHART -
LEARN HOW TO PLAY THE MOST COMMONLY PLAYED GUITAR CHORDS!

A CONVENIENTLY HANDY REFERENCE GUIDE FOR THE BEGINNING GUITAR PLAYER AND LOTS MORE!

COMING SOON!!...MORE COLORFUL SCALES, MODES, AND COMPLIMENTARY
CHORD PROGRESSIONS.....TO BE INTRODUCED IN A LATER GUITAR BOOK WHICH
WILL BE CALLED:

THE "ON STAGE" GUITAR BOOK -
LEARN HOW TO PLAY SCALE PATTERNS ON CHORDS EASILY & QUICKLY!

For more information about these other guitar learning items, visit Web Site at:

www.QUICKSTARTGUITAR.com

or write to:

Christopher Winkle Products
Attn: Chris Lopez
P.O. Box 1898
Lomita, CA 90717
USA

E-mail: quickstartguitar@msn.com

CUSTOMER MAIL-IN REVIEW PAGE
(Simply Remove This Page From Book And Mail)

We would appreciate hearing from you and knowing how you like the book.
Your review would be greatly appreciated.

We would like very much to have your review posted at various book selling locations.
Please fill out the following information and return to address indicated below.
You can also submit this information via E-mail at the address below.

Your Name:
Your Address:
City:
State: **Zip Code:**
Your E-mail Address:

It is necessary to include your E-mail address
Your E-mail address will not be posted when it is submitted to review locations

The "First Stage" Guitar Book.....
YOUR REVIEW & 5 STAR RATING:

WRITE A HEADLINE FOR YOUR REVIEW:

_____

YOUR REVIEW:

_____

_____

_____

_____

_____

Circle The Number You Rate This Book: **1 2 3 4 5**

(**1** Being The Lowest Rating & **5** Being The Highest Rating)

www.QUICKSTARTGUITAR.com

Please forward your review to this address:

Christopher Winkle Products
Attn: "QuickStartGuitar"
P.O. Box 1898
Lomita, CA 90717
USA

or

E-mail your review information to:

quickstartguitar@msn.com